More Than Names On A Wall

Remembering Bucks County's veterans who lost their lives serving our country during the Vietnam War.

A publication of

Doylestown Post 175, Veterans of Foreign Wars

Edited by James McComb

Cover art by Erin Williams

ISBN-13: 978-1466467545
ISBN-10: 1466467541

This book is dedicated to veterans everywhere.

Thank you for your service.

"Also I heard the voice of the Lord saying, whom shall I send, and who will go for us? Then said I, here am I; send me".

Isaiah 6: 8

… from this day to the ending of the world but we in it shall be remembered, we few, we happy few, we band of brothers. For he today that sheds his blood with me shall be my brother…

William Shakepeare
Henry V, Act 4 Scene 3

Dying for freedom isn't the worst thing that could happen – being forgotten is.

Unknown

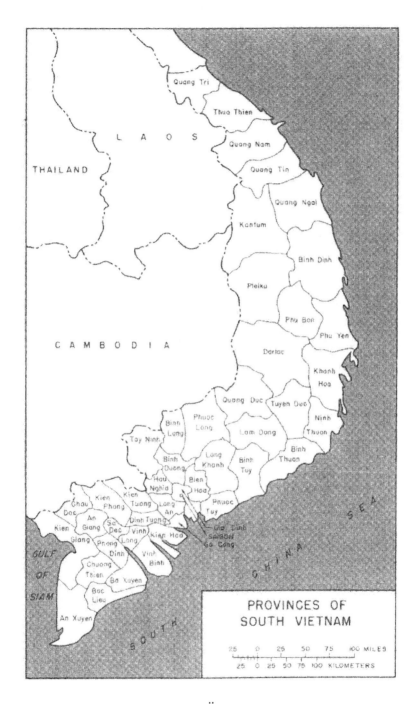

PROVINCES OF
SOUTH VIETNAM

ii

Contents

iv

v

Preface

If you were to stand in the courtyard on the south side of the Courthouse in Doylestown PA and look around you would see memorials to several wars – World War II, Korea, and the Persian Gulf. But if you would look due south, you would see the largest and most striking of the memorials – the Vietnam War Memorial. On this wall are inscribed the names of one hundred thirty three Bucks County residents who lost their lives serving our country during the Vietnam War. Also inscribed on this memorial are the names of three Bucks County men who were listed as Missing In Action. The remains of one of them have since been repatriated.

It is said that a man has not died as long as he is remembered. Each year a few weeks before Christmas, some Vietnam veterans and friends gather to decorate a Christmas tree in front of the Vietnam War Memorial. The decorations are red, white, and blue hearts each with the name of one of the one hundred thirty three Bucks County men who died while serving in Vietnam and the three men who are still listed as Missing In Action. In this most joyous time of the year we pause to honor their memory and to show that they are not forgotten. We move around the tree in a circular file with each person mounting an ornament of one of the men after his name has been announced. Thanks to the originators, Neil and Sherry Wolfe, this event has been taking place for over twenty years now. The ceremony concludes with all singing Silent Night. After last year's event my friend Rich and I walked away but we both acknowledged feeling this was not the end.

I am a native of Philadelphia and did not have the pleasure of knowing any of these men. The ceremony would have more meaning for me and most likely everyone, if we knew even a little about them. That was the genesis of this book. We

x

considered several options but we felt a book that could serve as a reference was the best option.

As I was putting this book together I collected the data on a spreadsheet. When reviewing the data the statistics become apparent. Their ages ranged from eighteen to forty one. Thirty percent were married, some had children. Sixty five percent were in the Army, twenty four percent in the Marines, and the rest were split almost equally between the Air Force and Navy. Twenty one percent were drafted. Their time in country ranged from a mere four days to five hundred fifty eight days. Seventy six percent died from hostile causes. But more than statistics, they were husbands, fathers, brothers, cousins, friends, etc. They all shared one thing in common – they rose to their country's call to duty and went to war. They did not return through any fault of their own. They deserve to be known as more than inscriptions on a wall and that was my purpose in putting this book together.

Having a full time job limits the time one has to pursue writing for pleasure. My intent was to compile as much information about each man that I could find with Internet research. Unfortunately, after 40+ years there is not as much information as I had hoped, especially photos. I attempted to correspond with friends and family of some of the guys but learned that many of the e-mail addresses used in the posting of remembrances were no longer valid. I did manage to contact some friends and family members but based on some responses, I felt I was re-opening wounds that had not quite healed so I abandoned that approach. The information presented here was primarily obtained from three excellent websites which are cited after each man's profile. I hope this is just the first edition of this book as I intend to continue researching these men and hopefully there will be subsequent editions, containing more information, in the not too distant future.

Jim McComb
USMC 1969 – 1973
Vietnam veteran 1970 – 1971
Past Commander – Doylestown Post 175 VFW

PS – here are a few notes that may help to provide a better understanding of this book:

1. Each man's rank is followed by his pay grade (E, O, or W and a number) and whether he Enlisted, was Drafted or was a Reserve.
2. MOS stands for Military Occupational Specialty. This was the job each man was trained to do.
3. The Republic of South Vietnam was divided into four tactical zones – I Corps, II Corps, III Corps and IV Corps. I Corps was the furthest north while IV Corps was the furthest south.
4. The last entry for each man is his location on The Wall. The Wall is the Vietnam Veterans Memorial in Washington, DC.

Foreword

What is a memorial? There are several definitions. The most appropriate is an object that serves as a focus for memory of something, usually a person or persons (who have died). It may be in the form of a landmark or an art object such as sculptures, statues or fountains, and even entire parks. A memorial can also be in the form of a tree, a medallion, or a memory. Anything that causes us to remember an event or a loved one can be thought of in this way.

For the 136 Bucks County Veterans who gave the ultimate sacrifice in Vietnam, that memorial is the Bucks County Pennsylvania Vietnam War Memorial. Dedicated on June 16, 1984, this monument displays the names of those who perished in Vietnam. A group of dedicated volunteers raised $250,000 over a four-and-a-half year period to secure the funding for the memorial, an effort, which consisted of more than 90 percent private fundraising.

Until now, the names were just an inscription on a wall. Each year in December, a group of dedicated Vietnam Veterans, their families and neighbors gather to hang an ornament bearing the names of those on that wall. It shows that these men will never be forgotten.

This work that you are holding in your hands that Jim painstakingly put together is a memorial to all of those on the Wall in Doylestown that have given their lives for their country. It was an unpopular war but its tolls were great. The pain never leaves those left behind and I hope this tribute brings to life the memories of the men the inscriptions represent.

With the publication of this work, those names are no longer just an inscription but have been given a face. With the work of its compiler and others, this work takes those names and adds that face with a description and account of their service.

Bob Staranowicz
VFW Post 175
US Army, 101st Airborne
Vietnam 1969-70

America's longest war was also its most divisive. The Vietnam War sadly ended the lives of 58,272 men and women serving in the United States Military. The conflict dramatically changed the lives of the more than 2.7 million American Servicemen and Servicewomen who served. Returning home to hateful and scornful crowds of young people who demeaned, defiled and despised them, these courageous veterans quietly resumed the lives that they had left. Their experiences, memories and pain were forced away to the deepest recesses of their minds, known only to them and to be recalled only by them. You see, no one really cared about them.

Vietnam Veterans learned from those who refused to separate the warrior from the war. Many protested sub-standard medical and mental health treatment. Many more demanded that their sacrifices and more importantly the sacrifices of those who were lost to the war in Vietnam be recognized. The courage, honor and commitment of those whose lives were cut sadly short pursuing the policy of the government of The United States would be recognized.

On the mall in Washington D.C. stands a stark monument known as the Vietnam Veterans Memorial. It is the most visited memorial on that mall. On it is inscribed, alphabetically in order of his or her death, the name of each of those 58,272. The memorial was dedicated on November 13, 1984.

In 1980, Mr. Dan Fraley a Bucks County citizen and United States Marine Vietnam Veteran envisioned and subsequently founded an organization that would build a similar memorial for those Bucks County citizens who had lost their lives in Vietnam. Dan's passion, persistence and professionalism ensured the completion of this memorial. There were dark moments. Dan has told me that there times when it seemed the money just was not there. Dan recently told me of a trip to the quarry that contracted to cut the stone for the memorial. They were afraid they would not be paid. Dan demonstrated his passion and dedication for the project; the stone was cut, shipped, inscribed and assembled to become The Bucks County Vietnam War Memorial. The memorial was dedicated on June 16, 1984.

The intention is to tell you, the reader a bit about those brave young men who left their lives in the jungles and hospitals of Vietnam. They were fathers, brothers, sons, uncles and friends. They most likely were known only to family and friends, but they most certainly were More Than Names On A Wall.

Rich Scott
United States Marine Vietnam Veteran

Acknowledgements

No one puts together a book without help and this book was no exception. Bill Severns, a retired Navy Chief and member of Post 175 contributed research data. Also assisting with research were two candidates for Post 175's college scholarship – Sarah Goetz and Jennifer Guidera, both students at Central Bucks High School East. My thanks go to another Post 175 member, Colonel Greg Marston, who included this as one of the scholarship projects.

My daughter, Erin Williams, although she doesn't know it, inspired me to write this book. Erin also designed the cover art. My friend and fellow Post 175 member Bob Staranowicz wrote one of the forewords and also provided helpful information on publishing a book. Bob had been through this process as he authored and published a novel entitled Chapter One. Another friend and fellow Post 175 member Rich Scott, also a Marine, wrote the other foreword and helped me with the concept of this book.

Commander Matt Fisher and the members of Post 175 provided the funding for the publishing and printing of this book and for that I am forever grateful.

I worked on this book almost every night for about nine months and must acknowledge my wife Sophie for her patience and support during this time.

Jim McComb
November, 2011

1963

Atis Karlis Lielmanis
(Quakertown)

United States Air Force
1st Air Commando Squadron, 34th Tactical Air Command,
13th Air Force
Recipient of the Air Force Cross and Air Medal

Rank: 1st Lieutenant (O-2), Reserve
MOS: 1585, Navigator
Born: January 2, 1939
Died: November 24, 1963
Circumstances: hostile; air loss or crash over land
Location: An Xugen Province (IV Corps Tactical Zone)
Marital Status: single
High School: Quakertown High School, class of 1957
Location on The Wall: panel 1E, line 34

Atis Lielmanis was originally from Latvia. From 1945 to 1950 he was in a displaced persons camp in Ansbah, West Germany. He immigrated to the United States in 1950.

In his high school yearbook, Atis is described as a gifted short story writer and artist. He was also outstanding in mathematics and sports but always found time for girls.

On 24 November 1963, a B-26B (tail number 44-35703) from the 1st Air Commando Squadron provided air support to ARVN troops operating south of Ca Mau in An Xugen Province. The ARVNSs were up against a well-armed and well dug-in VC force and were making little progress, impeded particularly by several machine gun emplacements. The B-26, crewed by Captain Howard R. Cody, 1st Lieutenant Atis K. Lielmanis, and a Vietnamese officer, made several attack runs against the machine guns. The VC responded by directing their fire against the B-26, thereby revealing their positions to other supporting aircraft – but 44-45703 was itself hit and on fire. Captain Cody broke off his attack and headed for the nearest runway, that at Ca Mau, but the B-26 went down about 24 kilometers south of Ca Mau. Ground impact was into the bank of a canal, where the forward part of the fuselage buried itself in the canal wall. Ground searches of the crash site were conducted between 25 and 27 November 1963 and the remains of two crewmen – 1st Lieutenant Lielmanis and the Vietnamese officer were recovered. Captain Cody's body was not found.

Citation for the Air Force Cross (awarded posthumously)

The Air Force Cross is presented to Atis Karlis Lielmanis, First Lieutenant, United States Air Force, for extraordinary heroism in military operations against an opposing armed force as an Advisor-Navigator of a B-26B aircraft on 24 November 1963. On that date, Lieutenant Lielmanis voluntarily exposed himself during a low level flight over hidden Viet Cong machine gun installations. Their fire badly damaged the aircraft, and it crashed, but this revealed the Viet Cong positions and resulted in their destruction by cover aircraft. Through his extraordinary heroism, superb airmanship, and aggressiveness in the face of hostile forces, First Lieutenant Lielmanis reflected the highest credit upon himself and the United States Air Force.

References:

http://www.virtualwall.org/dl/LielmanisAK01a.htm
http://www.thewall-usa.com/info.asp?recid=30606
http://www.vvmf.org/thewall/Wall_Id_No=30666

1965

Joseph Bradshaw Baggett
(Doylestown)

United States Air Force
4503rd Tactical Fighter Squadron, 3rd TAC FTR Wing,
13th Air Force
Recipient of the Air Medal

Rank: Major (O-4), Enlisted
Length of service: 12 years
MOS: 1115, Pilot
Born: April 18, 1930
Died: December 16, 1965
Age: 35
Circumstances: hostile; air loss or crash over land
Location: Gia Dinh Province (III Corps Tactical Zone)
Tour Started: October 23, 1965
Length of time in Vietnam: 54 days

Marital Status: married, 2 daughters, (Laura and Jennifer)
College: University of Florida and Syracuse University
Final resting place: Arlington National Cemetery
Location on The Wall: panel 4E, row 18

Family members said he was the first pilot to die while flying the F-5, a new plane he helped test for the Air Force and ended up following to Vietnam. Twelve of the planes were sent to Vietnam in the early days of the war.

Baggett's Air Force career began after a short stint at the University of Florida. It took him to Korea where he flew missions during the war, and later back to the United States to complete his bachelor's degree at Syracuse University in 1957.

He met his wife, Nancy, while both were living on an Air Force base in Suffolk County, England. They returned to the United States in 1961 to be married.

A former roommate of Joseph Baggett's at Syracuse reports that Baggett had been awarded the Distinguished Flying Cross after being shot down near Vladivostok, Russia during the Korean War. Apparently this award was not publicized as the circumstances were classified at that time.

References:

http://www.virtualwall.org/db/BaggettJB01a.htm
http://www.thewall-usa.com/info.asp?recid=1880
http://www.vvmf.org/thewall/Wall_Id_No=1915
http://www.arlingtoncemetery.net/jbbaggett.htm

Gregory Jeremicz
(Line Lexington)

United States Marine Corps
G Company, 2nd Battalion, 1st Marine Regiment,
1st Marine Division

Rank: Lance Corporal (E-3), Enlisted
MOS: 0311, Rifleman
Born: January 8, 1945
Died: December 18, 1965
Age: 20
Circumstances: hostile; ground casualty; multiple
fragmentation wounds
Location: Quang Nam Province (I Corps Tactical Zone)
Length of time in Vietnam: "about a year and a half"
Parents: John & Hildegarde
Marital Status: single
Religion: Roman Catholic
High School: North Penn High School
Location on The Wall: panel 4E, row 24

8

Gregory attended North Penn High School and worked as a carpenter's assistant before enlisting in the Marine Corps in October 1962. He served as a rifleman, maintenance man and, during his second tour in Vietnam, a military policeman with Company G of the 2nd Battalion, 1st Marines, 1st Marine Division. The 20-year-old lance corporal died on December 18, 1965, in Que Son, Quang Tin Province, during Operation Harvest Moon. Jeremicz was survived by his parents, four brothers and three sisters.

Originally Greg was interested in joining the Air Force. Because he dropped out of school he could not enlist in the Air Force so he joined the Marines. After his first tour in Vietnam he came home on leave and told his parents that he had enlisted because they needed him in Vietnam. He was on his second tour in Vietnam with only about three months to go when he was killed.

References:

http://www.virtualwall.org/dj/JeremiczGx01a.htm
http://www.thewall-usa.com/info.asp?recid=25870
http://www.vvmf.org/thewall/Wall_Id_No=25841
The Sunday Intelligencer, Vol. 96, No. 126, May 27, 1984

Fred Rost Tice
(Hilltown)

United States Air Force
35th Troop Carrier Squadron, 6315th Operations Group,
13th Air Force

Rank: Captain (0-3), Enlisted
Length of Service: 12 years
MOS: 1115, Pilot
Born: December 16, 1931
Died: September 18, 1965
Age: 33
Circumstances: Non-hostile, air loss or crash over land
Location: Binh Dinh Province (II Corps Tactical Zone)
Parents: Frank and Lorraine
Siblings: 1 sister (Susanna)
Marital Status: Married
High School: Hilltown High School, class of 1949
College: Penn State University, Bachelor of Science in
Aeronautical Engineering
Location on The Wall: panel 2E, row 89

Fred was based on Okinawa since November 1964. His wife
and children joined him there. He was a C-130 pilot who
regularly flew cargo missions to Vietnam. On September 18,
1965 Fred was co-pilot on a flight for Qui Nhon Air Base when

the aircraft was caught at low altitude by a severe downdraft. The plane went down several hundred feet short of the runway in 50 feet of water. Some of the crew escaped but Fred and the flight engineer drowned. His sister Susanna remarked "he died doing a job that he felt was worthwhile and doing what he liked best – flying." She also stated that Fred initially supported the US presence in Vietnam. He felt that US forces were doing the job that needed to be done.

References:
http://www.virtualwall.org/dt/TiceFR01a.htm
http://www.thewall-usa.com/info.asp?recid=52055
http://www.vvmf.org/thewall/Wall_Id_No=52032
The Sunday Intelligencer, Vol. 96, No. 126, May 27, 1984

Joseph Paul Yatsko Jr.

(Levittown)

United States Army
C Company, 2nd Battalion, 503rd Infantry, 173rd Airborne Brigade

Rank: 1st Lieutenant (O-2), Enlisted
Length of Service: 3 years
MOS: 71542, Infantry Unit Commander (Airborne Qualified)
Born: March 3, 1942
Died: December 18, 1965
Age: 23
Circumstances: Hostile; ground casualty, small arms fire
Location: Bien Hoa Province (III Corps Tactical Zone)
Tour Started: July 12, 1965
Length of time in Vietnam: 159 days
Marital Status: Married (Mary)

Religion: Roman Catholic
College: Appalachian State University
Final resting place: Beverly National Cemetery
Location on The Wall: panel 4E, row 27

He was a wrestler at Appalachian State University. He married the daughter (Mary) of a Colonel at Maguire Air Force Base. A ball field in Falls Township (Yatsko Field) is dedicated to his memory. He was known as the "Christmas Officer" of his outfit as he initiated Operation Christmas Vietnam which was a campaign with the folks back home, and Pennsbury High School, to send Christmas greetings to the members of his unit. After his death, his body was accompanied home by his brother Michael, a Corporal in Army also serving in Vietnam at the time.

References:
http://www.virtualwall.org/dy/YatskoJP01a.htm
http://www.thewall-usa.com/info.asp?recid=57765
http://www.vvmf.org/thewall/Wall_Id_No=57716

1966

Robert Lee Adams Jr.

(Levittown)

United States Army
C Company, 2nd Battalion, 27th Infantry Regiment,
25th Infantry Division

Rank: 2nd Lieutenant (O-1), Enlisted
Length of Service: 4 years
MOS: 1542, Infantry Unit Commander
Born: October 15, 1943
Died: November 4, 1966
Age: 23
Circumstances: hostile; ground casualty; gun or small arms fire
Location: Tay Ninh Province (III Corps)
Tour Started: September 30, 1966
Length of time in Vietnam: 35 days
Marital Status: married

14

Religion: Protestant
Final resting place: Arlington National Cemetery
Location on The Wall: panel 12E, row 16

References:
http://www.virtualwall.org/da/AdamsRL03a.htm
http://www.thewall-usa.com/info.asp?recid=229
http://www.vvmf.org/thewall/Wall_Id_No=271

Stanley Smith Cope Jr.
(Sellersville)

United States Marine Corps
2nd Platoon, H Company, 2nd Battalion, 26th Marine Regiment,
1st Marine Division

Rank: Private First Class (E-2), Drafted
Length of Service: less than 1 year
MOS: 0311, Rifleman
Born: October 2, 1946
Died: October 27, 1966
Age: 20
Circumstances: hostile, ground casualty; gun or small arms
fire
Location: Thua Thien Province (I Corps Tactical Zone)
Marital Status: single
Religion: Protestant
Final resting place: St. James Church Cemetery, Chalfont PA
Location on The Wall: panel 11E, row 118

Stanley is remembered by members of his unit as a gentle and
decent person – a little guy who had a smile for everyone. He

was killed during an ambush, during Operation Bacon, in the mountains west of the Hai Van Pass.

Editor's note: Operation Bacon took place in the Thua Thien Province over the period of October 19th to October 26th, 1966. Elements of the 26th Marine Regiment were involved.

References:
http://www.virtualwall.org/dc/CopeSS01a.htm
http://www.thewall-usa.com/info.asp?recid=10423
http://vvmf.org/thewall/Wall_Id_No=10434

John Francis Dalola III
(Penndel)

United States Army
173rd Engineering Company, 173rd Airborne Brigade

Rank: Private First Class (E-3), Enlisted
Length of Service: less than 1 year
MOS: 12A1P, Pioneer (Airborne qualified)
Born: October 1, 1947
Died: October 7, 1966
Age: 19
Circumstances: Hostile, ground casualty; explosive device while clearing a mine field
Location: not reported
Tour Started: June 15, 1966
Length of time in Vietnam: 114 days
Parents: James
Marital Status: Single
Religion: Roman Catholic
High School: Neshaminy High School
Location on The Wall: panel 11E, row 56

His parents received a letter from him the same day he was reported killed.

A street in Penndel is named after him.

References:
http://www.virtualwall.org/dd/DalolaJF01a.htm
http://www.thewall-usa.com/info.asp?recid=11771
http://www.vvmf.org/thewall/Wall_Id_No=11789

James Burkhardt Woot Detrixhe
(Fairless Hills)

United States Army
A Company, 2nd Battalion, 8th Cavalry Regiment,
1st Cavalry Division

Rank: Captain (O-3), Enlisted
Length of Service: 3 years
MOS: 71542, Infantry Unit Commander (Airborne qualified)
Born: November 25, 1940
Died: February 24, 1966
Age: 25
Circumstances: Hostile; ground casualty; gun or small arms fire
Location: not reported
Tour Started: August 2, 1965
Length of time in Vietnam: 206 days
Marital Status: married
Religion: Roman Catholic
Final resting place: Holy Savior Cemetery, Bethlehem PA
Location on The Wall: panel 5E, row 71

A member of his unit reports that while on patrol, the unit encountered heavy automatic weapons fire from an NVA force. Many Americans were immediately killed or wounded. Detrixhe went forward to recover a radio from a man who was down when he was killed. He had been the company commander for only a few days.

References:

http://www.virtualwall.org/dd/DetrixheJB01a.htm
http://www.thewall-usa.com/info.asp?recid=13039
http:/www.vvmf.org/thewall/Wall_Id_No=13072

Hugh William Elmore
(Eddington)

United States Army
C Company, 1st Battalion, 8th Cavalry Regiment,
1st Cavalry Division

18

Rank: Corporal (E-4), Enlisted
Length of Service: 1 year
MOS: 11C1P, Indirect Fire Infantryman (Airborne qualified)
Born: April 6, 1947
Died: March 25, 1966
Age: 18
Circumstances: hostile; ground casualty; misadventure
(friendly fire)
Location: Binh Duong Province (III Corps Tactical Zone)
Tour Started: August 20, 1965
Length of time in Vietnam: 217 days
Marital Status: single
Religion: Roman Catholic

Location on The Wall: panel 6E, row 48

Hugh Elmore grew up at St. John's and St. Vincent Orphan Asylums in Philadelphia. He had no family. A unit member reported that Elmore was working with the Mortar Platoon when an accident happened that took his life.

References:
http://www.VirtualWall.org/de/ElmoreHW01a.htm
http://www.thewall-usa.com/info.asp?recid=14992
http://www.vvmf.org/thewall/Wall_Id_No=14993

Carl Eugene Fell
(Bristol)

United States Army
A Company, 1st Battalion, 27th Infantry Regiment,
25th Infantry Division

Rank: Specialist 4th Class (E-4), Drafted
Length of Service: 1 year
MOS: 11B20, Infantryman
Born: April 11, 1943
Died: June 28, 1966
Age: 23
Circumstances: hostile; ground casualty; multiple fragmentation wounds
Location: Hau Nghia Province (III Corps Tactical Zone)
Tour Started: January 6, 1966
Length of time in Vietnam: 173 days
Marital Status: married
Religion: Protestant

Final resting place: Fletcher Cemetery, Monongalia WV
Location on The Wall: panel 8E, row 104

References:
http://www.VirtualWall.org/df/FellCE01a.htm
http://www.thewall-usa.com/info.asp?recid=15826
http://www.vvmf.org/thewall/Wall_Id_No=15827

Daniel A Hennessy
(Newtown)

United States Army
1st Platoon, B Company, 1st Battalion, 8th Cavalry Regiment,
1st Cavalry Division
Recipient of the Distinguished Service Cross

Rank: 1st Lieutenant (O-2), Reserve
Length of Service: 2 years
MOS: 71542, Infantry Unit Commander (Airborne Qualified)
Born: June 4, 1943
Died: December 28, 1966
Age: 23
Circumstances: hostile; ground casualty; gun or small arms fire
Location: Not reported
Tour Started: August 8, 1966
Length of time in Vietnam: 142 days
Marital Status: single
Religion: Roman Catholic
High School: Council Rock High School
Location on The Wall: panel 13E, row 91

Hennessy was posthumously awarded the Distinguished Service Cross. The citation reads:

The President of the United States takes pride in presenting the Distinguished Service Cross (Posthumously) to Daniel A. Hennessy (0-5326579), First Lieutenant (Infantry), U.S. Army, for extraordinary heroism in connection with military operations involving conflict with an armed hostile force in the Republic of Vietnam, while serving with Company B, 1st Battalion (Airborne), 8th Cavalry, 1st Cavalry Division (Airmobile). First Lieutenant Hennessy distinguished himself by exceptionally valorous actions on 28 December 1966 while serving as a platoon leader with elements of the 8th Cavalry n a search and destroy mission in Quan Hoai An Province. When his platoon suddenly received intense hostile fire from a nearby village, Lieutenant Hennessy dauntlessly led an assault on the Viet Cong positions. Maneuvering through a hail of bullets, hem moved to the head of the platoon and was the first man to enter the hamlet. Unmindful of his vulnerable position,

22

Lieutenant Hennessy fearlessly engaged the enemy with his rifle and hand grenades. He then called for artillery strikes within ten meters of his own position, which allowed his platoon to reach cover at the edge of a rice paddy. As he shouted orders and pointed out hostile emplacements, Lieutenant Hennessy was critically wounded by Viet Cong fire. Realizing that his wounds were fatal, he courageously continued to direct his men, until finally turning over command to his platoon sergeant with his last words. Demonstrating unimpeachable valor and profound concern for the men under his command, he inspired them to overwhelm and defeat the entrenched hostile force. First Lieutenant Hennessy's extraordinary heroism and devotion to duty, at the cost of his life, were in keeping with the highest traditions of the military service and reflect great credit upon himself, his unit, and the United States Army. Headquarters, US Army, Vietnam, General Orders No. 1658 (April 13, 1967)

Hennessy is remembered by his Company Commander as a great leader and superb soldier. He died leading his platoon into a fortified NVA village as Company B was in hot pursuit of the 22nd NVA regiment after their attack on LZ Pony. Although they made the 22nd NVA pay dearly, 13 men (including Hennessy) were lost that day.

Hennessy's medals are on display at his alma mater, Council Rock High School, to remind students of the sacrifices made by all who served in Vietnam.

References:
http://www.VirtualWall.org/dh/HennessyDA01a.htm
http://www.thewall-usa.com/info.asp?recid=22600
http://www.vvmf.org/thewall/Wall_Id_No=22583

Lee Edward Manning

(Bristol)

United States Navy
USS Blandy (DD-943)

Rank: Petty Officer 2nd Class (E-4)
MOS: Boiler Technician
Died: January 1966
Circumstances: The USS Blandy was cruising the Mediterranean when on January 27, 1966 one of the boilers blew up. Live steam was released into the boiler room where two sailors (one of which was Lee Manning) were standing watch. Both men were severely burned and med-evaced to the USS America. Both sailors died some time later.

Reference:
http://navysite.de/dd/dd943.htm

Randall Whit Moore

(Sellersville)

United States Army
A Company, 2nd Battalion, 327th Infantry Regiment,
101st Airborne Division

Rank: Private First Class (E-3), Enlisted
Length of Service: less than 1 year
MOS: 11B1P, Infantryman (Airborne Qualified)
Born: March 26, 1947
Died: November 8, 1966

Age: 19
Circumstances: Non-hostile, accidental self-destruction
Location: not reported
Tour Started: July 2, 1966
Length of time in Vietnam: 129 days
Parents: Dallas and Margaret (Robertson)
Marital Status: single
Religion: Protestant
Location on The Wall: panel 12E, row 43

References:
http://www.VirtualWall.org/dm/MooreRW01a.htm
http://www.thewall-usa.com/info.asp?recid=36222
http://www.vvmf.org/thewall/Wall_Id_No=34930

Robert Joseph Morris
(Oakford)

United States Army
3rd Platoon, B Company, 1st Battalion, 35th Infantry Regiment,
3rd Brigade, 25th Infantry Division

Rank: Private First Class (E-3), Enlisted
Length of Service: 1 year
MOS: 11B10, Infantryman
Born: December 27, 1947
Died: July 3, 1966
Age: 18
Circumstances: Hostile, gun or small arms fire
Location: Pleiku Province (II Corps Tactical Zone)
Tour Started: May 19, 1966
Length of time in Vietnam: 45 days

Parents: Robert and Emily (Westort)
Marital Status: single
Religion: Baptist
Final resting place: William Penn Cemetery, Somerton PA
Location on The Wall: panel 8E, row 125

His nickname was Moose and he was liked by everyone. He is remembered by his friends as a great guy with a terrific sense of humor.

References:
http://www.virtualwall.org/dm/MorrisRJ01a.htm
http://www.thewall-usa.com/info.asp?recid=36578
http://www.vvmf.org/thewall/Wall_Id_No=35285

Safford Smith Pye
(Levittown)

United States Army
A Company, 1st Battalion, 5th Infantry Regiment,
25th Infantry Division

Rank: Sergeant (E-5), Enlisted
Length of Service: 6 years
MOS: 11B40, Infantryman
Born: May 11, 1934
Died: February 11, 1966
Age: 31
Circumstances: hostile, gun or small arms fire
Location: not reported
Tour Started: January 6, 1966
Length of time in Vietnam: 36 days
Marital Status: married
Religion: Methodist
Location on The Wall: panel 5E, row 25

References:
http://www.VirtualWall.org/dp/PyeSS01a.htm
http://www.thewall-usa.com/info.asp?recid=41950
http://www.vvmf.org/thewall/Wall_Id_No=41968

Lawrence F Runey
(Bristol)

United States Army
A Company, 1st Battalion, 27th Infantry Regiment,
25th Infantry Division

Rank: 2nd Lieutenant (O-1), Enlisted
Length of Service: 1 year
MOS: 1542, Infantry Unit Commander
Born: September 21, 1941
Died: June 28, 1966
Age: 24
Circumstances: hostile, multiple fragmentation wounds
Location: Hau Nghia Province (III Corps Tactical Zone)
Tour Started: May 16, 1966

Length of time in Vietnam: 43 days
Marital Status: married, 1 daughter - Jane

Religion: Roman Catholic
College: Penn State University, ROTC
Final resting place: Beverly National Cemetery
Location on The Wall: panel 8E, row 105

References:
http://www.VirtualWall.org/dr/RuneyLF01a.htm
http://www.thewall-usa.com/info.asp?recid=44867
http://www.vvmf.org/thewall/Wall_Id_No=44877

John Francis Sanford

(Coopersburg)

United States Army
B Company, 1st Battalion, 327th Infantry Regiment,
101st Airborne Division

Rank: 1st Lieutenant (O-2), Reserve
Length of Service: 4 years
MOS: 71542, Infantry Unit Commander (Airborne qualified)
Born: February 19, 1942
Died: February 7, 1966
Age: 23
Circumstances: Hostile; ground casualty; gun or small arms fire
Location: Phu Yen Province (II Corps Tactical Zone)
Tour Started: January 14, 1966
Length of time in Vietnam: 24 days
Parents: Alden and Catherine (Cutler Ruggles)
Marital Status: single
Location on The Wall: panel 5E, row 15

On 07 Feb 1966 Company B, 1/327th Infantry, ran into a meat grinder in the tiny village of My Canh (2) in Phu Yen Province. As the men of B/1/327 approached the village they entered an area infested with mutually supporting, fortified, and camouflaged bunkers. In short order B/1/327 was pinned in place, unable to advance or retreat yet equally unable to stay where they were. A platoon from HQ Company, 1/327, was sent to flank and roll up the VC bunker line, succeeding only after bloody fighting.   earned a posthumous Medal of Honor by leading his troops

Although the combined force, with support from Allied air and artillery, was able to force the VC from the field, it was at high cost - B Co, 1/327, lost 19 men. 1st LT John Sanford, a

Platoon Leader in B/1/327, was among the 19 men from his company who died in the action.

References:
http://www.virtualwall.org/ds/SanfordJF01a.htm
http://www.thewall-usa.com/info.asp?recid=45497
http://www.vvmf.org/thewall/Wall_Id_No=45506

Editor's note:
It is the editor's policy to list the home towns of each man as they appear on the memorial in Doylestown. Errors will be noted but not corrected. Coopersburg is actually located in Lehigh County not Bucks County.

Walter W. Shipley Jr.
(Bristol)

United States Army
2nd Platoon, C Troop, 1st Squadron, 4th Cavalry Regiment, 1st Infantry Division

Rank: Staff Sergeant (E-6), Enlisted
Length of Service: 10 years
MOS: 11E40, Armor crewman
Born: December 14, 1936
Died: August 25, 1966
Age: 29
Circumstances: hostile, ground casualty, gun or small arms fire
Location: Binh Duong Province (III Corps Tactical Zone)
Tour Started: July 29, 1966
Length of time in Vietnam: 27 days
Marital Status: married
Religion: Episcopal
Location on The Wall: panel 10E, row 44

References:
http://www.virtualwall.org/ds/ShipleyWW01a.htm
http://www.thewall-usa.com/info.asp?recid=47219
http://www.vvmf.org/thewall/Wall_Id_No=47219

John William Thomas

(Levittown)

United States Army
C Company, 1st Battalion, 503rd Infantry Regiment,
173rd Airborne Brigade

Rank: Specialist 4th Class (E-4), Enlisted
Length of Service: 4 years
MOS: 11B2P, Infantryman (Airborne qualified)
Born: February 22, 1942
Died: January 10, 1966
Age: 23
Circumstances: hostile; ground casualty; gun or small arms fire
Location: Binh Duong Province (III Corps Tactical Zone)
Tour Started: November 8, 1965
Length of time in Vietnam: 63 days
Marital Status: single
Religion: Lutheran
Location on The Wall: panel 4E, row 62

References:
http://www.virtualwall.org/dt/ThomasJW02a.htm
http://www.thewall-usa.com/info.asp?recid=51677
http://www.vvmf.org/thewall/Wall_Id_No=51658

Rodney Gardner Thornton
(Croydon)

United States Marine Corps
3rd Platoon, F Company, 2nd Battalion, 9th Marine Regiment,
3rd Marine Division

Rank: Sergeant (E-5), Enlisted
Length of Service: 6 years
MOS: 0311, Rifleman
Born: January 19, 1941
Died: October 5, 1966
Age: 25
Circumstances: hostile, multiple fragmentation wounds
Location: Quang Tri Province (I Corps Tactical Zone)
Tour Started:
Length of time in Vietnam:
Marital Status: married to Alice; 1 son (Patrick), 1 daughter
(Mary)
Religion: Mormon
Location on The Wall: panel 11E, row 50

Rodney Thornton was the Platoon Sergeant of 3rd Platoon. He
is remembered by his fellow platoon members as a no
nonsense leader who was a Marine's Marine. He led from the
front.

References:
http://www.virtualwall.org/dt/ThorntonRG01a.htm
http://www.thewall-usa.com/info.asp?recid=51999
http://www.vvmf.org/thewall/anClip=152471

Edward Alfred Wellings
(Warrington)

United States Marine Corps
C Company, 1st Battalion, 4th Marine Regiment,
3rd Marine Division

Rank: Private First Class (E-2), Enlisted
Length of Service: 1 year
MOS: 0311, Rifleman
Born: December 14, 1943
Died: September 21, 1966
Age: 22
Circumstances: hostile, ground casualty, gun or small arms fire
Location: Quang Tri Province (I Corps Tactical Zone)
Tour Started: unknown
Length of time in Vietnam: unknown
Marital Status: single

Religion: Protestant
Parents: Mr. & Mrs. George A. Wellings
Final resting place: Philadelphia National Cemetery, Philadelphia PA
Location on The Wall: panel 10E, row 129

He was known as Eddie to his companions but Skipper to his family. While visiting San Diego, California in May of 1965, Eddie enlisted in the Marine Corps. He went to basic training in San Diego. He was wounded in August and had only recently returned to his unit when he met his death. His sister remembers him as one who never complained.

Edward Wellings is one of the three namesakes of Igoe Porter Wellings Park in Warrington.

In an interview conducted in 1984, George Wellings recalled that if there was any trouble his son was right in the middle of it. Edward enlisted in the Marine Corps at the age of 21 while

he was supposedly on vacation in California. Edward's last visit home was in July and August of 1966 while he was on leave recovering from being wounded by gunfire. After his leave, Edward returned to his unit at Quang Tri and was again wounded on August 24, 1966 while taking part in a search and destroy mission with the 4th Marines. He was struck in the head by gunfire and died on September 21 from those wounds.

References:
http://www.virtualwall.org/dw/WellingsEA01a.htm
http://www.thewall-usa.com/info.asp?recid=55214
http://www.vvmf.org/thewall/Wall_Id_No=55173
The Sunday Intelligencer, Vol. 96, No. 126, May 27, 1984

1967

Karol Raymond Bauer
(Wrightstown)

United States Marine Corps
M Company, 3rd Battalion, 3rd Marine Regiment,
3rd Marine Division

Rank: Staff Sergeant (E-6), Enlisted
Length of Service: 10 years
MOS: 0369, Infantry Unit Leader
Born: June 26, 1938
Died: April 30, 1967
Age: 28
Circumstances: hostile, ground casualty, other explosive device
Location: Quang Tri Province (I Corps Tactical Zone)
Tour Started: unknown
Length of time in Vietnam: unknown
Marital Status: married to Mary Jacqueline (Creaven), 1 daughter
Religion: Roman Catholic

38

High School: Olney High School
Final resting place: Thompson Memorial Church Cemetery, New Hope PA
Location on The Wall: panel 18E, row 118

The career Marine Corps non-commissioned officer enlisted in 1956 after leaving Olney High School. He later obtained a high school diploma in the service. Bauer, 28, died on April 30, 1967, as he led a platoon of Company M, 3rd Battalion, 3rd Marines, 3rd Marine Division, at Khe Sanh, Quang Tri Province. Bauer's wife was a former Woman Marine.

In early April the North Vietnamese Army's 325C Division (18th, 95th, and 101st Regiments) moved through Laos and positioned itself to capture the combat base at Khe Sanh. By 25 April the 18th Regiment had emplaced itself on Hill 861, one of three hills which controlled key terrain around Khe Sanh. The 3rd Marine Division commander determined that the three hills had to be denied to the enemy.

After heavy fighting, the Marines captured Hill 661, decimating the 18th Regiment, and turned toward Hills 881 North and 881 South, defended by the NVA 95th Regiment.

The initial assault on Hill 881 South was made by elements of the 3rd and 9th Marines on 30 April and was not successful - the enemy was well entrenched on the crest of the steep hill and vigorously resisted the Marine advance. By nightfall, the Marines withdrew from the hill, having lost 57 dead and hundreds wounded. Hill 881 South was subjected to heavy supporting arms fire on 01 May and captured on 02 May.

Staff Sergeant Karol R. Bauer was killed in action during the initial assault on 30 April.

References:
http://www.virtualwall.org/db/BauerKR01a.htm
http://www.thewall-usa.com/info.asp?recid=2904
http://www.vvmf.org/thewall/Wall_Id_No=2907

James Edward Boorman
(Hulmeville)

United States Army
B Company, 2nd Battalion, 47th Infantry Regiment,
9th Infantry Division

Rank: Sergeant (E-5), posthumously promoted, Drafted
Length of Service: less than 1 year
MOS: 11B40, Infantryman
Born: August 11, 1946
Died: April 27, 1967
Age: 20
Circumstances: hostile, ground casualty, gun or small arms fire
Location: Tay Ninh Province (III Corps Tactical Zone)
Tour Started: January 10, 1967
Length of time in Vietnam: 107
Marital Status: single
Religion: Methodist
Location on The Wall: panel 18E, row 100

References:
http://www.virtualwall.org/db/BoormanJE01a.htm
http://www.thewall-usa.com/info.asp?recid=4739
http://www.vvmf.org/thewall/Wall_Id_No=4763

Edward Soliz Cantu
(Bristol)

United States Army
Headquarters & Headquarters Company, 2nd Battalion,
503rd Infantry Regiment, 173rd Airborne Brigade

Rank: Specialist 4th Class, (E-4), Enlisted
Length of Service: 2 years
MOS: 91B2P, Medical NCO (Airborne qualified)
Born: February 28, 1947
Died: November 20, 1967
Age: 20
Circumstances: hostile, ground casualty, gun or small arms fire
Location: Kontum Province (II Corps Tactical Zone)
Tour Started: October 16, 1967
Length of time in Vietnam: 35 days
Marital Status: married
Religion: Roman Catholic
Final resting place: Resurrection Cemetery, Cornwells Heights, PA
Location on The Wall: panel 30E, row 38

References:
http://www.virtualwall.org/dc/CantuES01a.htm
http://www.thewall-usa.com/info.asp?recid=7750
http://www.vvmf.org/thewall/Wall_Id_No=7768

Hopson Covington
(Bristol)

United States Army
A Company, 2nd Battalion, 22nd Infantry Regiment,
25th Infantry Division

Rank: Private First Class (E-3), Drafted
Length of Service: less than 1 year
MOS: 11B10, Infantryman
Born: October 20, 1943
Died: December 29, 1967 (incident date was December 15, 1967)
Age: 24
Circumstances: hostile, ground casualty, other explosive device
Location: Tay Ninh Province (III Corps Tactical Zone)
Tour Started: August 21, 1967
Length of time in Vietnam: 130 days
Marital Status: married, 2 daughters, Brenda and Lisa
Religion: Protestant

High School: Delhaas High School
Final resting place: Philadelphia United Methodist Church Cemetery, Rockingham NC
Location on The Wall: panel 32E, row 91

His nickname was Sneak-a-Peak. He was originally from Rockingham NC but had lived in Bristol most of his life.

References:
http://www.virtualwall.org/dc/CovingtonHx01a.htm
http://www.thewall-usa.com/info.asp?recid=10728
http://www.vvmf.org/thewall/Wall_Id_No=10738

Theodore H. Davis
(Neshaminy)

United States Army
A Company, 4th Battalion, 9th Infantry Regiment, 25th Infantry Division

Rank: Staff Sergeant (E-6), Enlisted
Length of Service: 16 years
MOS: 11B40, Infantryman
Born: March 27, 1934
Died: February 26, 1967
Age: 32
Circumstances: hostile, ground casualty, gun or small arms fire
Location: Binh Duong Province (III Corps Tactical Zone)
Tour Started: February 5, 1967
Length of time in Vietnam: 21 days
Marital Status: married
Religion: Methodist

Final resting place: Fort Riley Post Cemetery
Location on The Wall: panel 15E, row 95

References:
http://www.virtualwall.org/dd/DavisTH01a.htm
http://www.thewall-usa.com/info.asp?recid=12340
http://www.vvmf.org/thewall/Wall_Id_No=12348

David John Decker
(Yardley)

Capt. David J. Decker—Pennsylvania

United States Army
B Company, 2nd Battalion, 8th Cavalry Regiment,
1st Cavalry Division

Rank: Captain (O-3), Enlisted
Length of Service: 8 years
MOS: 1542, Infantry Unit Commander
Born: August 30, 1937
Died: November 19, 1967
Age: 30
Circumstances: hostile, ground casualty, gun or small arms fire
Location: Kontum Province (II Corps Tactical Zone)
Tour Started: June 28, 1967
Length of time in Vietnam: 144 days
Marital Status: married
Religion: Roman Catholic
Final resting place: Arlington National Cemetery
Location on The Wall: panel 30E, row 24

Captain Decker is remembered by those who served under him as a good man whose only fault was that he cared too much for his men. He died trying to save one of his men who had been captured by the NVA.

References:
http://www.virtualwall.org/dd/DeckerDJ01a.htm
http://www.thewall-usa.com/info.asp?recid=12551
http://www.vvmf.org/thewall/Wall_Id_No=12723

Theodore Aloyis Dougherty
(Cornwells Heights)

United States Army
E Company, 3rd Battalion, 60th Infantry Regiment,
9th Infantry Division

Rank: Sergeant (E-5), Enlisted
Length of Service: 18 years
MOS: 11B40, Infantryman
Born: November 11, 1926
Died: November 24, 1967
Age: 41
Circumstances: hostile, ground casualty, multiple
fragmentation wounds
Location: Dinh Tuong Province (IV Corps Tactical Zone)
Tour Started: May 21, 1967
Length of time in Vietnam: 187 days
Marital Status: single
Religion: Roman Catholic
Location on The Wall: panel 30E, row 76

Dougherty first enlisted, in the Army in 1944, at the age of 18 and was wounded, during World, War II. He also served in combat during the Korean War. As a squad leader he was assigned to Company A, of the 3rd, Battalion, 60th, Infantry, 9th Infantry Division. He was wounded in the arm and leg in August of 1967. He returned to this unit after his recuperation. He was previously wounded in Korea by a dynamite blast and ''ared some vision impairment as a result. His final wound ''asult of a booby trap in the Mekong Delta region.

rphan and had lived at St. Vincent's Orphan st. Joseph's House for Boys (both in Philadelphia) .g to St. Francis Home for Boys in Bensalem. After .1e orphanages, he graduated from St. Francis .1al School in Bensalem and worked for a truck body r in Jenkintown and also for the Nabisco Bakery in .delphia.

References:
http://www.virtualwall.org/dd/DoughertyTA01a.htm
http://www.thewall-usa.com/info.asp?recid=13777
http://www.vvmf.org/thewall/Wall_Id_No=13779

Clay Edward Downey Jr.
(Bristol)

United States Army
B Company, 2nd Battalion, 5th Cavalry Regiment,
1st Cavalry Division

Rank: Sergeant (E-5), Enlisted
Length of Service: 2 years

MOS: 11B20, Infantryman
Born: August 16, 1946
Died: February 12, 1967
Age: 20
Circumstances: hostile, ground casualty, gun or small arms fire
Location: Binh Dinh Province (II Corps Tactical Zone)
Tour Started: September 9, 1966
Length of time in Vietnam: 156 days
Marital Status: single
Religion: Roman Catholic
Final resting place: Beverly National Cemetery. Buried alongside his father, Private Clay Edward Downey Sr, US Army.
Location on The Wall: panel 15E, row 19

References:
http://www.virtualwall.org/dd/DowneyCE01a.htm
http://www.thewall-usa.com/info.asp?recid=13834
http://www.vvmf.org/thewall/Wall_Id_No=13836

Allan George Griffin

(Buckingham)

United States Army
A Company, 1st Battalion, 2nd Infantry Regiment, 1st Infantry Division

Recipient of the Bronze Star with V for Valor

Rank: Private First Class (E-3), Drafted
Length of Service: less than one year
MOS: 11B10, Infantryman

Born: December 10, 1943
Died: February 22, 1967
Age: 23
Circumstances: non-hostile, ground casualty, accidental homicide
Location: unknown
Tour Started: January 7, 1967
Length of time in Vietnam: 46 days
Parents: Mr. and Mrs. Carl L.
Marital Status: single
Religion: Lutheran
Location on The Wall: panel 15E, row 74

His niece recalls that he was awarded the Bronze Star with V for valor.

References:
http://www.virtualwall.org/dg/GriffinAG01a.htm
http://www.thewall-usa.com/info.asp?recid=20041
http://www.vvmf.org/thewall/Wall_Id_No=20030

Geoffrey Lawrence Ham
(Ivyland)

United States Army
A Company, 2nd Battalion, 12th Cavalry Regiment,
1st Cavalry Division

Rank: 1st Lieutenant (O-2), Reserve
Length of Service: 1 year
MOS: 1542, Infantry Unit Commander
Born: January 30, 1943

Died: June 28, 1967
Age: 24
Circumstances: hostile, ground casualty, gun or small arms fire
Location: Kontum Province (II Corps Tactical Zone)
Tour Started: March 4, 1967
Length of time in Vietnam: 116 days
Parents: Donald and Edna (Parker)
Marital Status: single
High School: Lower Moreland High School
College: Temple University
Final resting place: Kensico Cemetery, Valhalla NY
Location on The Wall: panel 22E, row 78

Former classmates of his at Temple recall Geoff was an outstanding student, a varsity championship, an extraordinary leader and a true gentleman. He was a cheerful fellow to be around - poised, well liked, handsome and squared away. Even then he was a model of what a future Army officer should be.

A former neighbor remembers him as a young, vivacious individual who loved life and his country.

References:
http://www.virtualwall.org/dh/HamGL01a.htm
http://www.thewall-usa.com/info.asp?recid=20922
http://www.vvmf.org/thewall/Wall_Id_No=20908

William Harry Haworth
(Bristol)

United States Army
E Company, 15th Combat Engineer Battalion,
9th Infantry Division

Recipient of the Bronze Star with V for Valor

Rank: Sergeant (E-5) posthumous promotion, Enlisted
Length of Service: 1 year
MOS: 12C20, Bridge Crewman
Born: July 30, 1946
Died: May 25, 1967
Age: 20
Circumstances: hostile, ground casualty, multiple fragmentation wounds
Location: Long An Province (III Corps Tactical Zone)
Tour Started: October 1, 1966
Length of time in Vietnam: 236 days
Marital Status: single
Religion: Roman Catholic
Final resting place: Beverly National Cemetery
Location on The Wall: panel 20E, row 103

Haworth was killed when the bridge truck in which he was riding struck a mine. The explosion blew the bed of the truck off and onto him. He was med-evaced out but lived only another 8 hours. He had talked to other members of his unit about becoming a priest. He was awarded the Bronze Star with V for Valor.

References:
http://www.virtualwall.org/dh/HaworthWH01a.htm
http://www.thewall-usa.com/info.asp?recid=22070
http://www.vvmf.org/thewall/Wall_Id_No=22053

David Herman Holland

(Springtown)

United States Marine Corps
K Company, 3rd Battalion, 9th Marine Regiment,
3rd Marine Division

Rank: Private First Class (E-2), Enlisted
Length of Service: less than 1 year
MOS: 3041, Supply Administrative Man
Born: May 27, 1948
Died: May 21, 1967
Age: 18
Circumstances: hostile, ground casualty, gun or small arms fire
Location: Quang Tri Province (I Corps Tactical Zone)
Tour Started: unknown
Length of time in Vietnam: unknown
Parents: Herman and Ethel (Snyder)
Siblings: 1 sister
Marital Status: single
Religion: Lutheran
High School: Palisades High School
Final resting place: Springtown Cemetery, Springtown PA
Location on The Wall: panel 20E, row 74

His high school track coach remembers him as a great athlete.

References:
http://www.virtualwall.org/dh/HollandDH01a.htm
http://www.thewall-usa.com/info.asp?recid=23731
http://www.vvmf.org/thewall/Wall_Id_No=23710

William John Igoe
(Warrington)

United States Army
A Troop, 1st Squadron, 4th Cavalry Regiment,
1st Infantry Division

Recipient of the Distinguished Service Cross

Rank: Private First Class (E-3), Drafted
Length of Service: 1 year
MOS: 11D10, Armor Reconnaissance Specialist
Born: October 15, 1946
Died: July 11, 1967
Age: 20

Circumstances: hostile, ground casualty, burns
Location: Binh Long Province
Tour Started: March 14, 1967
Length of time in Vietnam: 119 days
Parents: Thomas & Elizabeth (Graham)
Marital Status: single
Religion: Roman Catholic
High School: Central Bucks High School
College: Penn State University
Final resting place: Resurrection Cemetery, Cornwells Heights
Location on The Wall: panel 23E, row 52

He was known as Bill to his friends and family. He was a center for the varsity football team. He had completed one year at Penn State University and worked as a cost estimator at Link Belt in Colmar prior to joining the Army.

Bill was awarded the Distinguished Service Cross posthumously.

Citation: The President of the United States takes pride in presenting the Distinguished Service Cross (Posthumously) to William John Igoe (US52674743), Private First Class, U.S. Army, for extraordinary heroism in connection with military operations involving conflict with an armed hostile force in the Republic of Vietnam, while serving with Troop A, 1st Squadron, 4th Cavalry, 1st Infantry Division. Private First Class Igoe distinguished himself by exceptionally valorous actions on 11 July 1967 while serving as a machine gunner on an Armored Assault Vehicle. In the early morning hours, his base camp was attacked by a large enemy force firing mortars, recoilless rifles, automatic weapons and explosive charges. From the outset, Private Igoe poured heavy fire into the attacking insurgents killing many and preventing penetration of his portion of the perimeter. When an enemy force succeeded in breaking through another portion of the defenses, he continued his accurate fire though wounded by mortar fragments. As the battle progressed, an explosive charge was thrown into the assault vehicle but was deflected by Private Igoe. The ensuing explosion seriously wounded him and set the vehicle afire, but he continued to fire on the attackers while directing the other members of the crew to escape. As the men were leaving, a recoilless rifle round hit the vehicle and mortally wounded Private Igoe. His courageous actions in warning his comrades before the final explosion undoubtedly saved their lives. Private First Class Igoe's extraordinary heroism and devotion to duty, at the cost of his life, were in keeping with the highest traditions of the military service and reflect great credit upon himself, his unit, and the United States Army. Headquarters, US Army, Vietnam, General Orders No. 4429 (August 30, 1967) Home Town: Warrington, Pennsylvania

William is one of the three namesakes of Igoe Porter Welling Park in Warrington

References:
http://www.virtualwall.org/di/IgoeWJ01a.htm
http://www.thewall-usa.com/info.asp?recid=25049
http://www.vvmf.org/thewall/Wall_Id_No=25024

George Harry Johnson
(Croydon)

United States Marine Corps
D Company, 1st Battalion, 7th Marine Regiment,
1st Marine Division

Rank: Corporal (E-4), Enlisted
Length of Service: 1 year
MOS: 0311, Rifleman
Born: August 28, 1948
Died: June 3, 1967
Age: 18
Circumstances: hostile, ground casualty, gun or small arms fire
Location: Quang Tin Province (I Corps Tactical Zone)
Tour Started: unknown
Length of time in Vietnam: unknown
Marital Status: single
Religion: Roman Catholic
Final resting place: Resurrection Cemetery, Cornwells Heights
Location on The Wall: panel 21E, row 47

References:
http://www.virtualwall.org/dj/JohnsonGH01a.htm
http://www.thewall-usa.com/info.asp?recid=26166
http://www.vvmf.org/thewall/Wall_Id_No=26136

Robert Warren Meiss Jr.

(Yardley)

United States Marine Corps
K Company, 3rd Battalion, 9th Marine Regiment,
3rd Marine Division

Rank: Corporal (E-4), Enlisted
Length of Service: 3 years
MOS: 0311, Rifleman
Born: January 11, 1946
Died: May 20, 1967
Age: 21
Circumstances: hostile, ground casualty, artillery, rocket or mortar
Location: Quang Tri Province (I Corps Tactical Zone)
Tour Started: unknown
Length of time in Vietnam: unknown
Marital Status: married to Katie (Schlussler)
Religion: Protestant
High School: Pennsbury High School, class of 1964
Final resting place: Ewing Cemetery Chapel, Trenton NJ
Location on The Wall: panel 20E, row 64

Robert is remembered by a high school classmate as a guy with a friendly manner and an easy smile. A former member of his unit in Vietnam recalls him as a good person and a good Marine. He had a positive attitude and was always there for his friends.

References:
http://www.virtualwall.org/dm/MeissRW01a.htm
http://www.thewall-usa.com/info.asp?recid=34703
http://www.vvmf.org/thewall/Wall_Id_No=33415

57

Walter F. Morris

(Penndel)

United States Army
178th Assault Support Helicopter Company, 14th Aviation
Battalion, 1st Aviation Brigade

Recipient of the Distinguished Flying Cross and Air Medal

Rank: Chief Warrant Officer (W-2), Reserve
Length of Service: 3 years
MOS: 062D, Helicopter Pilot, Medium Transport
Born: June 27, 1943
Died: April 26, 1967
Age: 23
Circumstances: hostile, died of wounds, air loss or crash over land. Morris was piloting a CH-47B Chinook helicopter and was shot and killed by small arms fire while approaching at Danang.
Location: Quang Nam Province (I Corps Tactical Zone)
Tour Started: September 17, 1966
Length of time in Vietnam: 221 days
Marital Status: married, 1 son - Walter
Final resting place: Resurrection Cemetery, Cornwells Heights, PA
Location on The Wall: panel 18E, row 95

References:
http://www.virtualwall.org/dm/MorrisWF01a.htm
http://www.thewall-usa.com/info.asp?recid=36587
http://www.vvmf.org/thewall/Wall_Id_No=35294

Frederick Albert Newby Jr.
(Feasterville)

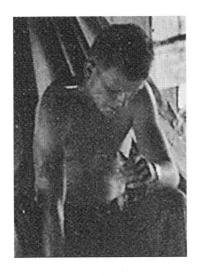 

United States Marine Corps
K Company, 3rd Battalion, 7th Marine Regiment,
1st Marine Division

Rank: Lance Corporal (E-3), Enlisted
Length of Service: 1 year
MOS: 0311, Rifleman
Born: July 12, 1946
Died: August 6, 1967
Age: 21
Circumstances: hostile, ground casualty, gun or small arms fire
Location: Quang Nam Province (I Corps Tactical Zone)
Tour Started:
Length of time in Vietnam:
Marital Status: single
Religion: Roman Catholic
High School: Lincoln High School, Philadelphia PA

Final resting place: Beverly National Cemetery
Location on The Wall: panel 24E, row 84

"War is hell and it's getting worse every minute," wrote Newby in his last letter home from Vietnam. In the same letter, he told his youngest sister how to take care of a music box he had sent for her birthday. After graduating from high school he worked as a tool and die maker for Bachman Brothers on East Erie Avenue. The son of a World War II veteran who saw action in the South Pacific, he enlisted in the Marine Corps on February 5, 1966. He was stationed at Guantanamo Bay, Cuba, for five months before being sent to Vietnam.

References:
http://www.virtualwall.org/dn/NewbyFA01a.htm
http://www.thewall-usa.com/info.asp?recid=37719
http://www.vvmf.org/thewall/Wall_Id_No=37751

Douglas Arthur Post
(Richboro)

United States Navy
USS Forrestal, VF-74, TF77, CVW-17,
7th Fleet

Rank: Airman (E-3), Reserve
Length of Service: 2 years
MOS: unknown
Born: December 27, 1945
Died: July 29, 1967
Age: 21
Circumstances: non-hostile, casualty at sea, died in the fire
on the USS Forrestal
Location: Gulf of Tonkin
Marital Status: single
Religion: Protestant
High School: Council Rock High School
Location on The Wall: panel 24E, row 40

On 29 July 1967 the USS FORRESTAL was operating on Yankee Station off the coast of North Vietnam conducting combat operations. This was the fifth such day of operations and at 10:52am the crew was starting the second launch cycle of the day, when suddenly a Zuni rocket accidentally fired from an F-4 PHANTOM into a parked and armed A-4 SKYHAWK. The accidental launch and subsequent impact caused the belly fuel tank and a 1,000 pound bomb on the Skyhawk to fall off, the tank broke open spilling JP5 (jet fuel) onto the flight deck and ignited a fire. Within a minute and a half the bomb was the first to cook-off and explode, this caused a massive chain reaction of explosions that engulfed half the air wing's aircraft, and blew huge holes in the steel flight deck. Fed by fuel and bombs from other aircraft that were armed and ready for the coming strike, the fire spread quickly, many pilots and support personnel were trapped and burned alive. Fuel and bombs spilled into the holes in the flight deck igniting fires on decks further into the bowels of the ship.

Berthing spaces immediately below the flight deck became death traps for fifty men, while other crewmen were blown overboard by the explosion. Nearby ships hastened to the FORRESTAL's aid. The ORISKANY (CV 34), herself a victim of a tragic fire in October 1966, stood by to offer fire-fighting and medical aid to the larger carrier. Nearby escort vessels sprayed water on the burning FORRESTAL and within an hour the fire on the flight deck was under control. The crew heroically fought the fire and carried armed bombs to the side of the ship to throw them overboard for 13 hours. Secondary fires below deck took another 12 hours to contain. Once the fires were under control, the extent of the devastation was apparent. Most tragic was the loss to the crew, 134 had lost their lives, while an additional 64 were injured, this was and still remains the single worst loss of life on a United States

Navy vessel since the USS FRANKLIN (CV 13) was bombed in WW II

References:
http://www.virtualwall.org/dp/PostDA01a.htm
http://www.thewall-usa.com/info.asp?recid=41355
http://www.vvmf.org/thewall/Wall_Id_No=41376

Patrick Robert Roy
(Levittown)

United States Army
C Company, 1st Engineering Battalion,
1st Infantry Division

Rank: Private First Class (E-3), Drafted
Length of Service: 1 year
MOS: 12A10, Pioneer

Born: May 24, 1947
Died: December 16, 1967
Age: 20
Circumstances: non-hostile, ground casualty, vehicle loss or crash
Location: Binh Duong Province (III Corps Tactical Zone)
Tour Started: October 30, 1967
Length of time in Vietnam: 47 days
Marital Status: single
Religion: Roman Catholic
Final resting place: Beverly National Cemetery
Location on The Wall: panel 32E, row 12

References:
http://www.virtualwall.org/dr/RoyPR01a.htm
http://www.thewall-usa.com/info.asp?recid=44703
http://www.vvmf.org/thewall/Wall_Id_No=44713

Alan Robert Schultz
(Levittown)

United States Marine Corps
F Company, 2nd Battalion, 9th Marine Regiment,
3rd Marine Division

Rank: Lance Corporal (E-3), Enlisted
Length of Service: 1 year
MOS: 3041, Supply Administrative Man
Born: March 4, 1947
Died: August 11, 1967
Age: 20

Circumstances: hostile, ground casualty, artillery, rocket or mortar
Location: Quang Tri Province (I Corps Tactical Zone)
Tour Started: not reported
Length of time in Vietnam: unknown
Marital Status: single
Religion: Roman Catholic
High School: Pennsbury High School
Final resting place: Our Lady of Grace Cemetery, Penndel PA
Location on The Wall: panel 24E, row 101

Alan is remembered by a high school classmate as a body builder who also ran track and always had a big, infectious grin. The brother of a former girlfriend remembers him as a guy who made him feel like a million bucks because Alan would talk to him and show him things. The brother also remembers Alan as a fine young man, noble, kind and courageous. Alan did not have to join the service as he had an older brother in the Air Force but he joined the Marines anyway.

References:
http://www.virtualwall.org/ds/SchultzAR01a.htm
http://www.thewall-usa.com/info.asp?recid=46168
http://www.vvmf.org/thewall/Wall_Id_No=46174

Robert L. Scott Jr.
(Churchville)

United States Army
176th Attack Helicopter Company, 14th Aviation Battalion,
17th Aviation Group, 1st Aviation Brigade

65

Rank: Warrant Officer (W-1), Reserve
Length of Service: less than 1 year
MOS: 062B, Helicopter Pilot, Utility and Light Cargo Single Rotor
Born: September 20, 1947
Died: August 25, 1967
Age: 19
Circumstances: hostile, air loss or crash over land
Location: Quang Tin Province (I Corps area)
Tour Started: August 11, 1967
Length of time in Vietnam: 14 days
Marital Status: single
Religion: Baptist
High School: Council Rock High School
Location on The Wall: panel 25E, row 44

References:
http://www.virtualwall.org/ds/ScottRL03a.htm
http://www.thewall-usa.com/info.asp?recid=46392
http://www.vvmf.org/thewall/Wall_Id_No=46395

Ronald James Siengo

(Cornwells Heights)

United States Army
3rd Platoon, C Company, 2nd Battalion, 35th Infantry Regiment,
4th Infantry Division

Rank: 2nd Lieutenant (O-1), Reserve
Length of Service: 2 years
MOS: 1542, Infantry Unit Commander
Born: January 17, 1946
Died: Monday, December 25, 1967
Age: 21
Circumstances: hostile, ground casualty, misadventure
(friendly fire)
Location: Quang Ngai Province (I Corps Tactical Zone)
Tour Started: November 15, 1967
Length of time in Vietnam: 40 days

Marital Status: single
Religion: Roman Catholic
High School: Bensalem High School, class of 1965
College: University of West Virginia
Final resting place: Beverly National Cemetery
Location on The Wall: panel 32E, row 60

Second Lt. Ronald J. Siengo, was killed Christmas Day when hit by mortar fire near the Demilitarized Zone. His body was found two days later. Lt. Siengo had been planning to marry Carol Welter of Newtown, upon completion of his Army service November 15. His brother, 2d Lt. David Siengo, said Ronald and Miss Welter had known each other for more than 10 years.
A 1965 graduate of Bensalem High School, Lt. Siengo had been active in sports, particularly football. He was an avid hunter and fisherman who, while on leave last October won a trophy for killing the largest deer with bow and arrow in Bucks County. The trophy was to have been awarded Sunday, December   31,   1967.

After high school, Lt. Siengo enlisted in the Army and served at various military installations.   While in the service he attended the University of West Virginia for a year. He was admitted to Officers Candidate School, which he attended at Fort Benning, Ga., with his brother. He graduated on April 4, 1967. Lt. Siengo arrived in Vietnam on December 1. He was originally assigned to the 9th Infantry Division and then transferred to the 4th Infantry Division as a rifle platoon leader. On a tape he recorded for his parents amid the crashes of a mortar attack, he told his family of the hardships incurred by the Vietnamese people and how they were under clothed and underfed. His brother recalled the recording: "He said he had a job to do and was doing it the best he knew how."

References:

http://www.virtualwall.org/ds/SiengoRJ01a.htm
http://www.thewall-usa.com/info.asp?recid=47419
http://www.vvmf.org/thewall/Wall_Id_No=47417

Harry Jennings Simmons Jr.
(Langhorne)

United States Marine Corps
E Company, 2nd Battalion, 1st Marine Regiment,
1st Marine Division

69

Rank: Lance Corporal (E-3), Enlisted
Length of Service: less than 1 year
MOS: 0311, Rifleman
Born: December 21, 1946
Died: April 8, 1967
Age: 20
Circumstances: hostile, ground casualty, gun or small arms fire
Location: Quang Nam Province (I Corps Tactical Zone)
Parents: Harry and Frances (Chase)
Marital Status: single
High School: Neshaminy High School
Final resting place: Sunset Memorial Park, Feasterville PA
Location on The Wall: panel 17E, row 129

Simmons was a member of a fire team operating near Da Nang at the time of his death. He attended Neshaminy High School and enlisted in July 1966. He was scheduled for home leave in December and planned to marry his fiancé of two years, Barbara Reingold, of Levittown.

References:
http://www.virtualwall.org/ds/SimmonsHJ02a.htm
http://www.thewall-usa.com/info.asp?recid=47543
http://www.vvmf.org/thewall/Wall_Id_No=47540

Ralph Wentz Smith
(New Britain)

United States Marine Corps
15th Counter Intelligence Team, Headquarters Company, Headquarters Battalion, 3rd Marine Division

Recipient of the Bronze Star (Korean War)

Rank: Gunnery Sergeant (E-7), Enlisted
Length of Service: 20 years
MOS: 0811, Field Artillery Cannoneer
Born: November 14, 1929
Died: June 2, 1967
Age: 37
Circumstances: hostile, ground casualty, other explosive device
Location: Quang Tri Province (I Corps Tactical Zone)
Tour Started: unknown
Length of time in Vietnam: unknown
Parents: Edward (deceased) and Ruth
Siblings: 4 brothers (Walter, Wilbur, Harold, and Robert) and 1 sister (Katherine)
Marital Status: married, 5 children
Religion: Protestant
High School: Doylestown High School
Final resting place: 29 Palms Cemetery, 29 Palms CA
Location on The Wall: panel 21E, row 39

Ralph was due to retire from the Marine Corps in November 1967.

References:
http://www.virtualwall.org/ds/SmithRW03a.htm
http://www.thewall-usa.com/info.asp?recid=48510
http://www.vvmf.org/thewall/Wall_Id_No=48504

Robert Harold Smith

(Warminster)

United States Army
A Battery, 2nd Battalion (Aerial Rocket Artillery),
20th Artillery Regiment, 1st Cavalry Division

Recipient of the Air Medal

Rank: Specialist 4th Class (E-4), Drafted
Length of Service: 1 year
MOS: 45J20, Aircraft Armament Repairman
Born: October 27, 1946
Died: January 24, 1967
Age: 20
Circumstances: hostile, air loss or crash over land
Location: Binh Dinh Province (II Corps Tactical Zone)
Tour Started: September 25, 1966
Length of time in Vietnam: 121 days
Parents: Allen and Anna
Marital Status: single
Religion: Protestant
High School: William Tennent High School, class of 1965
Final resting place: Pine Grove Cemetery, Warminster PA
Location on The Wall: panel 14E, row 73

Robert was a crew chief with the Flying Falcons, a helicopter combat team. His helicopter was shot down by hostile automatic weapons ground fire.

References:
http://www.virtualwall.org/ds/SmithRH02a.htm
http://www.thewall-usa.com/info.asp?recid=48545
http://www.vvmf.org/thewall/Wall_Id_No=48537

Frank Herbert Thomas Jr.
(Levittown)

United States Marine Corps
I Company, 3rd Battalion, 9th Marine Regiment,
3rd Marine Division

Rank: Private First Class (E-2), Enlisted
Length of Service: less than 1 year
MOS: 0311, Rifleman
Born: January 18, 1947
Died: March 30, 1967
Age: 20
Circumstances: hostile, ground casualty, artillery, rocket, or mortar
Location: Quang Tri Province (I Corps Tactical Zone)
Tour Started: unknown
Length of time in Vietnam: unknown
Marital Status: single
Religion: Roman Catholic
Location on The Wall: panel 17E, row 76

Frank remembered by his squad leader as a good Marine. He was killed while he and his fire team were protecting a rocket team from attacking NVA during the "Battle of Getlin's Corner" on March 30, 1967. His unit was outnumbered many times over but managed to repulse the attack several times.

References:

http://www.virtualwall.org/dt/ThomasFH01a.htm
http://www.thewall-usa.com/info.asp?recid=51624
http://www.vvmf.org/thewall/Wall_Id_No=51606

John Kirby Williams
(New Britain)

United States Navy
D Company, Naval Mobile Construction Battalion-1,
3rd Naval Construction Brigade

Rank: Steel Worker 3rd Class (E-4), Reserve
Length of Service: 3 years
MOS: Steel Worker Erector
Born: June 21, 1943
Died: August 9, 1967
Age: 24
Circumstances: hostile, ground casualty, other explosive device
Location: Quang Tri Province (I Corps Tactical Zone)
Parents: James and Rose
Marital Status: single
Religion: Roman Catholic
High School: Mercy Technical High School
Final resting place: unknown
Location on The Wall: panel 24E, row 98

John joined the Navy in March 1966. He loved sports, especially scuba diving, and spent many days diving in quarries and lakes in Pennsylvania and New Jersey.

References:
http://www.virtualwall.org/dw/WilliamsJK02a.htm
http://www.thewall-usa.com/info.asp?recid=56357
http://www.vvmf.org/thewall/Wall_Id_No=56314

Harry Conrad Wilson II
(Richboro)

United States Army
173rd Engineering Company, 173rd Airborne Brigade

Rank: Specialist 4th Class (E-4), Enlisted
Length of Service: 1 year
MOS: 11B10, Infantryman
Born: December 23, 1946
Died: November 18, 1967
Age: 20
Circumstances: hostile, ground casualty, multiple
fragmentation wounds
Location: Kontum Province (II Corps Tactical Zone)
Tour Started: January 16, 1967
Length of time in Vietnam: 306 days

Marital Status: single
Religion: Presbyterian
High School: Council Rock High School, class of 1966
Location on The Wall: panel 30E row 21

References:
http://www.virtualwall.org/dw/WilsonHC01a.htm
http://www.thewall-usa.com/info.asp?recid=56711
http://www.vvmf.org/thewall/Wall_Id_No=56667

Kenneth Glen Worman
(Perkasie)

United States Army
3rd Platoon, B Company, 1st Battalion, 35th Infantry Regiment,
25th Infantry Division

Recipient of the Bronze Star with V for valor

Rank: Private First Class (E-3), Drafted
Length of Service: less than 1 year
MOS: 11B10, Infantryman

Born: April 21, 1947
Died: May 22, 1967
Age: 20
Circumstances: hostile, ground casualty, multiple
fragmentation wounds
Location: Quang Ngai Province (I Corps Tactical Zone)
Tour Started: February 27, 1967
Length of time in Vietnam: 84 days
Parents: Glenn and Viola (Cressman)
Marital Status: single
Religion: Protestant
High School: Pennridge High School, class of 1966
Final resting place: Whitemarsh Memorial Park, Prospectville
PA
Location on The Wall: panel 20E, row 88

References:
http://www.virtualwall.org/dw/WormanKG01a.htm
http://www.thewall-usa.com/info.asp?recid=57438
http://www.vvmf.org/thewall/Wall_Id_No=57392

1968

William James Barr
(Warminster)

United States Navy
MILPHAP Team 6

Rank: Hospitalman
Length of Service: 1 year
MOS: Hospital Corpsman
Born: September 22, 1948
Died: July 16, 1968
Age: 19
Circumstances: non-hostile, ground casualty, malaria
Location: Gia Dinh Province (III Corps Tactical Zone)
Tour Started: March 22, 1968
Length of time in Vietnam: 116 days
Parents: George and Marjorie (Miller)
Marital Status: single
High School: William Tennant High School, class of 1966

Final resting place: Sunset Memorial Park, Feasterville PA
Location on The Wall: panel 52W, row 38

The editors contacted William Barr's sister Patrice. This is what she wrote about her brother:

This will be difficult. It's been more than forty years since I last saw my brother alive. I was only twelve. Little did I know that within less than a year I'd be around 30.

I know that my brother died a man. Who could spend so much as one hour in that place and not transform instantly from boy to man?

But most of my memories are not of Hospitalman William James Barr. I remember my brother, Billy. To me, he became a hero and shall forever remain larger than life. Billy graduated in 1966, from William Tennent High School, in Warminster. He joined the Navy in that same year.

Billy joined the Navy in order to "avoid" being drafted. The draft meant having no choice about the job. Billy knew he would serve, but never wanted to hurt or kill another human being. He enlisted to be a Corpsman so he could save lives and not have to take them.

He was a typical, freckled faced, "All American Kid". He was funny. He was kind. He was, for a time, a member of a local volunteer fire department. He came home from one fire with a broken heart because they'd not been able to save the dog.

We used to joke about his freckles. We'd tease that he must have stood behind a screen door to get a tan. Just like the brothers on The Wonders Years, my brothers and I fought like cats and dogs – but only with each other. He and I were especially close, even though he was so many years older than I was. I guess that's the benefit of having been the only sister.

He's the one who knew I talked in my sleep. He knew all my secrets. He never told. He never even blackmailed me.

The freckly, goofball who was my brother went away to the Navy. Around Christmas, 1967, he came home approximately 8 feet taller. He came to pick me up from school, wearing his Marine uniform. (Much more manly than a sailor suit, I guess.) He patiently allowed me to parade him around to show him off. The girls went more than a little ga-ga.

He was the first male human being to tell me I was pretty. He was the first person to talk to me as though I was an intelligent grown-up. He took the time to make me feel special. Pretty remarkable stuff from a kid sister's perspective. He gave me a "grown up" present for Christmas that year. A silver rose (pin). It's one of the few things from that long ago I have managed to not lose.

He told me one day, during his last visit home, that he didn't expect to come back alive. Not in a whiney, snively, scared-half-to-death sort of way. Just something he "knew". I don't think he told anybody else. I'm not sure and am certainly not going to ask anybody else in the family. He was only there for four months. With a Marine unit, somewhere in the jungle.

The mail being what it was in those days, I don't recall getting many letters addressed specifically to me. It never occurred to me that he wouldn't come home, so I didn't have the sense to save them.

The one thing that has always stuck with me. He told me that he hadn't understood why we were there until he got there. Having seen the suffering of the Vietnamese people, he said he did understand. He was proud to be there and believed he was doing something good.

I know there had to have been much more to it than that. He kept a diary, but my parents burned it. I have a lot of unanswered questions about the person he was while he was there. I'm content with my memories.

I have never met or heard from anybody from his unit. I hope they thought as highly of him as he did of them.

He rests in Sunset Memorial Park. I don't know the grave number or location. I have not been back there, but for once during the first year after he died. (I don't need to visit his grave. He has been with me every day.)

I'm also a Veteran. I served in the Army from July, 1974 – January, 1980. They issued me an NDSM. I wore my brother's. I wore it proudly. I named my son after him.

When he died, they flew flags at half-mast in our town. Fire trucks were in the funeral procession, carrying the flowers.

You'd have liked Billy. Most people did.

"I'm the One Called "Doc..."

I shall not walk in your footsteps,
but I will walk by your side.
I shall not walk in your image,
I've earned my own title of pride.
We've answered the call together,
on sea and foreign land.
When the cry for help was given,
I've been there right at hand.
Whether I am on the ocean
or in the jungle wearing greens,
Giving aid to my fellow man,
be it Sailors or Marines.
So the next time you see a corpsman

and you think of calling him "squid",
Think of the job he's doing
as those before him did.
And if you ever have to go out there
and your life is on the block,
Look at the one right next to you...
I'm the one called "Doc".

Harry D. Penny, Jr. HMC(AC)USN
Copyright 1975

"Permission to reprint granted
by the author/copyright owner".
(Permission for both poem & graphic)

References:
http://www.virtualwall.org/db/BarrWJ01a.htm
http://www.thewall-usa.com/guest.asp?recid=2617
http://www.vvmf.org/thewall/Wall_Id_No=2620

Warren Martin Beaumont

(Langhorne)

United States Army
A Company, 2nd Battalion, 22nd Infantry Regiment,
25th Infantry Division

Rank: Private First Class (E-3), Enlisted
Length of Service: 1 year
MOS: 11B10, Infantryman
Born: November 24, 1948
Died: April 12, 1968 (Good Friday)
Age: 19
Circumstances: hostile, ground casualty, artillery, rocket, or mortar
Location: Tay Ninh Province (III Corps Tactical Zone)

Tour Started: March 15, 1968
Length of time in Vietnam: 28 days
Marital Status: single
Religion: Methodist
High School: Neshaminy High School, class of 1966
Final resting place: Arlington National Cemetery
Location on The Wall: panel 49E, row 28

The editors contacted a former squad mate of Beaumont's.
Here is what he wrote:

*Warren came to my squad in March of 68, and we became
friends immediately. He was from Neshaminy High school and
I went to Easton High school in Easton, so we were about 25
or 30 miles apart. We called him Sonny along with another guy
that came in with him that we called Pops. Pops was about 25
years old with a master's degree in math, but his deferment
ran out and he was thrust into the infantry. Sonny was a quick
learner and caught on fast. We enjoyed talking trash about
each other's high schools since we were big rivals in football.
One day we were on patrol along a river and a col. in a
chopper spotted some VC. along the river banks and told our
CO to check it out. So we were dispatched to look for them. I
was walking in the river chest deep with my claymore bags
filled with magazines for my M16 when I stepped into a deep
hole and went straight down. I had to get rid of all my weight or
I was done. As I came to the surface I realized I'm heading
downstream. Sonny grabbed an overhanging tree branch and
stuck his legs out for me to grab onto, thus saving my ass. I
lost everything, my ammo, M16, and my glasses which I'm
blind as a bat without. Never did find the VC.*

*We were a mechanized unit ,Co. A, 2nd battalion 22nd Inf.
with the 25th Inf. Div. As we set up that night on a road we had
to set out our LP posts. I was scheduled to go out on LP, but*

had to stay in that night because of losing my glasses in the river. Sonny and Pops both went out on that LP, I don't remember which one took my place but to this day it still haunts me as they were both killed that night.

 I try to post messages on The Wall-USA for all my 25th Inf. Brothers that appear on the wall. I got a response a few years ago from Sonny's old high school girlfriend. She told a little about him and sent pictures of his grave. He is buried in Arlington National Cemetery, I have been down to see him many times along with a few others that I know. Sonny's girlfriend started dating a Vietnam Vet and they went to visit his grave and she about had a heart attack. Here the guy she was dating was in our old outfit in Nam. She felt Sonny had come back to her thru this guy.

References:
http://www.virtualwall.org/db/BeaumontWM01a.htm
http://www.thewall-usa.com/info.asp?recid=3113
http://www.vvmf.org/thewall/Wall_Id_No=3116

Edward Nelson Beers
(Fairless Hills)

United States Marine Corps
K Company, 3rd Battalion, 1st Marine Regiment,
1st Marine Division

Rank: Lance Corporal (E-3), Enlisted
Length of Service: 1 year (enlisted March 1967)
MOS: 0311, Rifleman
Born: November 25, 1947
Died: May 23, 1968
Age: 20
Circumstances: hostile, ground casualty, other explosive device (fragmentation bomb)

Location: Quang Tri Province, Hill 512 (I Corps Tactical Zone)
Tour Started: August 15, 1967
Length of time in Vietnam: 282 days
Marital Status: single
Religion: Protestant
High School: Pennsbury High School, class of 1965
Location on The Wall: panel 66E, row 6

A former squad mate of Edward Beers wrote:

Edward always had a way, of making you smile, even in the worst of times. I met Ed, in November, of 1967. He was a friendly sort, always smiling. I remember him as always liking the 'oldies but goodies' - he would sing that melody all the time. He was good at making a bad situation easier to cope with. I was with him the day he died. We were a few miles from Khe Sanh. He was hit with artillery, he was pretty messed up, but we thanked God, that he went fast, no suffering. The way we all wanted to go if we had to. I remember, when he came back from Bangkok on R&R, all he talked, about for weeks, were cheeseburgers and cokes. Him and I got more mail then anyone. When mail came in, they would send either Ed or me to get it seeing we were the only ones who got mail. Sometimes ten to twenty letters at one mail call. We all missed him very much, his funny laugh, jokes, singing and dirty blond hair that was always, falling in front of his face. But in spite of all the laughter, when the shit, hit the fan (and it did,) he was always right there. He was a good man, to have on your side, Edward was truly a hero. We were only together for months but I remember him fondly today.

A close friend of his remembers:

Ed was quite a guy. We hung out at the bowling alleys next to his dad's gas station on Newportville Road. He was reluctant to go with us anywhere in fear of disappointing his dad. But we still had fun at the station and Reenees Pizza. Ed was hard working and had a heart the size of the moon.

Beers' father said his letters always mentioned his desire to return home and work in the family service station at Emilie and Oxford Valley rds. in Bristol township. One letter, scrawled on a C-ration container, was written in Pennsylvania Dutch dialect, which Beers learned in Vietnam from a friend. It read in part: "Ik wil naar huis gan." Beers' parents are Pennsylvania Dutch and they translated it as this: "I'll be home soon." They thought it good news.

References:
http://www.virtualwall.org/db/BeersEN01a.htm
http://www.thewall-usa.com/info.asp?recid=3250
http://www.vvmf.org/thewall/Wall_Id_No=3253

Steven Michael Bezenski

(Levittown)

United States Army
Headquarters and Headquarters Company, 55th Medical Group, 44th Medical Brigade

Rank: Specialist 5th Class (E-5), Drafted
Length of Service: 1 year
MOS: 71B30, Clerk Typist
Born: October 25, 1945
Died: Tuesday, March 26, 1968
Age: 22
Circumstances: non-hostile, ground casualty, illness or disease

91

Location: Binh Dinh Province (II Corps Tactical Zone)
Tour Started: June 5, 1967
Length of time in Vietnam: 295 days
Marital Status: single
Religion: Roman Catholic
High School:
College:
Final resting place: Resurrection Cemetery, Bensalem PA
Location on The Wall: panel 46E, row 29

References:
http://www.virtualwall.org/db/BezenskiSM01a.htm
http://www.thewall-usa.com/info.asp?recid=3882
http://www.vvmf.org/thewall/Wall_Id_No=3909

William Warren Breece Jr.
(Yardley)

United States Army
A Troop, 7th Squadron, 1st Cavalry Regiment,
1st Aviation Brigade

Recipient of the Silver Star and Air Medal

Rank: Warrant Officer (W-1), Reserve
Length of Service: less than 1 year
MOS: O62B, Helicopter Pilot
Born: May 3, 1948
Died: Thursday, December 5, 1968
Age: 20
Circumstances: William Warren Breece, Jr, was the co-pilot
of an OH-6A helicopter (hull number 66-07892). Breece was
hit by enemy small arms fire while making a firing run against

enemy troops. The pilot made a precautionary landing to allow first aid, but Breece died of his injuries.

Location: Kien Giang Province (IV Corps Tactical Zone)
Tour Started: October 27, 1968
Length of time in Vietnam: 39 days
Parents: Mr. and Mrs. William
Siblings: 1 brother (Jim)
Marital Status: single
Religion: Presbyterian
High School: Pennsbury High School, class of 1966
College: Ball State College, Muncie IN
Final resting place: Newtown Cemetery, Newtown PA
Location on The Wall: panel 37W, row 45

He was called Warren by his friends. He is remembered by a childhood friend who wrote:

I knew Warren as a young boy in my hometown of Morrisville Pennsylvania. His nickname was "Ogre", he was a big fellow. I was a kid of around 8-9 I suppose when I last saw him, I guess he just kind of "disappeared" into the Army without any fanfare. He hung around with my buddy's older brothers, the Schmitt kids. His folks owned a florist/nursery, or he worked there maybe as I recall. As big a bruiser as Warren was, I remember him as a gentle giant. Where the other older kids could get mean and rough with us little guys, he always was quiet and reserved. I remember my mom crying when she heard he had died in Viet Nam,,I don't recall at the time it really hitting me,,not like it is now, some 30+ years later. I served 21 years in the Air Force and whenever I think of Viet Nam I think of Warren Breece. Right now, Warren I am crying for you brother. God Bless you for ensuring my childhood was a good one and that I now raise my children in the rich blessings of liberty. .

The editors contacted another childhood friend, Tommy Schmitt. He wrote a tribute to his friend that we have included in its entirety because it speaks to all who are in this book.

This is indeed a grateful tribute to a soldier and friend that has passed in service to the United States of America and as a way of us remembering a teenage friend that was out to raise hell and make something of himself.

We met I do not know for sure but it was in the year of 1964 when we were in junior high school together at Boehm Jr. High-Yardley, Pa. Our town was a small up and coming town (Yardley) in Bucks County Pennsylvania. We had a pizzeria and a florist. Warren's dad owned and operated the florist. Warren was the older of two boys born to a wonderful Mom and Dad. I'll forever call them Mr. and Mrs. Breece out of respect which Mrs. Breece has become my Mom over the last 42 years since Warren died after being shot down on December 5 1968 in Vietnam.

Being always in the need for companionship as young men are......always looking for beer (at age 16 was normal) and motorcycles and of course the girls were too complicated to handle.......we stayed together on occasion looking into open garages for beer. My brothers ......there were 4 of us and of course Warren normally gravitated to us for a little hell raising. So as it turns out he was the instigator on a lot of our shenanigans.

One special 1964 story was up the road from our neighborhood was a new water tank, just recently built to provide water for the rapidly growing Bucks County; the tank sat on a hill and overlooked our entire town, from the outskirts of Newtown (Pa. where Warren was to be laid to rest a short four years later), to the Skudders Falls Bridge (over the Delaware river) down river to Morrisville (Pa. where we had the funeral for Warren on Friday, December 13, 1968) and over to our high school (Pennsbury-Fairless Hills, Pa.). You could see forever.......Warren sure liked heights and he proved it that night. Well as boys will be boys, Warren sure wanted to follow us up there to the top of the tank. You must remember the tank was a new empty tank and very eerier than all get out as we climbed the ladder with every step making a clanging sound as we got higher. Boy guess what, Warren was not to be shown up by the "small fries" (we were all (4 boys-shorter and much smaller than Warren) so Warren had to get to the top first. Well guess again, he got to the top but we could not resist throwing rocks at the tank every time he tried to start to get back on the ladder to come down. And we would not let up throwing the stones. Finally as boys will be boys we had played a good one on him as he was again first to the top and could not get down with the rocks clanging the eeriest sound you can imagine on the empty tank every time he stepped on the ladder. Turns out we just left him there and departed for home. Boy he sure was mad but in fact did show us who was the first to the top. We were always envious of our Warren. By the way his (very private) nickname was "Oger" as he was so big and towered over us small fries. We sure would like to see him again and reminisce about our tank story. But he never got a chance, but we know he got to the TOP in Vietnam just four years later. Our hero, true hero as I share this story with you as I type this, the tears do run. I miss him so. It has been since 1964 to now.......2011, 47 years, boy how the time passes with good memories of our fallen.

Guess this is a good time to mention; why this is written. As with great sense of loss, I recall the young man that went to war and did not come back. It is truly a loss that cannot be expressed completely. Suffice to say when my successes are measured because it was because of the life that was given to make me strong. In remembering Warren I am stronger because he was the strong, always the "Oger" getting to the TOP for all of us left to grow up, which he never had a chance to do. He represents why I made it; because he got to the TOP first.

Continuing Warren's story; we all graduated from Pennsbury in 1966 and went on to better things. Warren went to Ball State College (Muncie, Indiana) for a year. This is where you must remember the summer of 1966 when Warren met Pam. Well was she special. Warren had his motorcycle and hit the road. All the way to Orono Maine where he met Pam. That is Pam Ware a very special lady that was the best thing to get Warren to the TOP. Again, he had it all the TOP girl, a TOP motorcycle and acceptance to the TOP Military Helicopter Flight Training there is. I do not know all the details but Warren and Pam were sweethearts. I will only suffice to add a comment from Pam attached which shows her feelings after to many years (45+) as an attachment to this story.

Well as you may well know the Vietnam Draft was the main subject and at the height of all the minds of us teenagers. So to bet that you must know that Warren did enlist for United States Army Warrant Officer Flight School. He was accepted in the winter of 1967 and preceded to Mineral Wells, Texas as a Warrant Officer Candidate (WOC) for Helicopter Primary Flight Training. Boy, were we boys envious; again Warren was getting to the TOP first. His high school grades were always better than us boys. Warren's Mom was always getting him to get the homework done, which paid off in Flight Training. I capitalize all mention of the military here out of respect and not the English punctuation and of course respect for Mrs. Breece. Upon graduation he spend (his last) month or so with Pam and us 4 boys. This was a time of great pride for Warren and his family. Distinguished Graduate from a Military Flight School; fantastic again Warren at the TOP.

To continue from here is with great difficulty, as this is the point in the story where none of us at home (USA) ever see Warren alive again. PCS is short for Permanent Change of

Station in military terms; Warren had just graduated from the TOP helicopter flight school in the world, now his PCS deployment sent him to his death in the Republic of Vietnam. As I can remember our last serious talk together just down the road from his father's Yardley Florist Shop, the discussion went something like this: I asked, what will happen if you die? His reply was a matter of fact; "then shit happens" were his last words to me on this subject. Now 43 years later, those words ring in my memory as the words in the clear tone of a true hero. He was going over there to do a matter of fact job and that was how he looked at it. Risk was a matter of fact for a hero and he accepted it that way. A twenty year old hero, how in the world can the young know and except life from that age as a matter of fact. I will always hold true those words from Warren -"then shit happens". Here I share 42 years of true grit words that formed my character as I drew very vivid memories from that day when again Warren was on TOP knowing what a 20 year old WO-1 (Warrant Officer-One; U.S. Army rank) had achieved. Warren's words hold true as the primary origin of my successful 38 year military career.

Receiving a single letter from Warren, which I will share only with his family, Warren had many comments on the helicopter missions, which resulted in many successes. He had volunteered for scout duty. You may ask – what is a Scout, but I am sure everybody knows that the scout is the one who is up front as point man looking from initial contact, only he did it from the air. As a new WO-1 in country Warren was on TOP again, out front looking for the bad guys. He found them on 05 Dec 1968 and the story goes like this. The following as described to me (in 2005) by the pilot flying with him at the time 1st LT Roy Ferguson:

> "Warren was in the left seat of our OH-6A aircraft, we had been looking at grass top level, only the grass was about 8 feet high, when all of a sudden we were

confronted with a group of North Vietnamese Army (NVA) troops who instead of running away from us did in fact turned around and started shooting at us. We were doing a speed greater than them so we made a go around to get into better position for our mini-gun to be used. On several passes at the enemy, Warren continually was firing his M-16 through the left side in literally one on one contact at short range of the NVA. The mini-gun was ablaze as we engaged them with literally a water hose effect of white hot metal bullets. It lasted only a few seconds as the NVA had again turned and shot Warren."

"The bullet had entered his under arm and exited his forehead. He was slumped forward on the controls as his Ogre size body was so confined in the Scout cockpit. As a result the aircraft skidded to a halt from that low altitude. From our crash landing, I did my best to return fire but with minimal effect till help came. The NVA stayed put and returned fire until our attack aircraft assisted. The AH-1G Cobra gun-ship helicopters formed a racetrack pattern which after what seemed eternity, allowed us some reprieve so we could get Warren evacuated. He was taken immediately to a field hospital with no chance at life. He had done his duty".

Again on TOP of it all, out in front, up there doing what needed to be done. Some gave………… Warren gave all.

His body was returned expedited home and with church services in on Friday 13 December 1968, in Morrisville Pennsylvania, following by internment. Full military honors were accorded as Warren was laid to rest in the Newtown Cemetery off of the Yardley-Newtown Road, Newtown, Bucks County Pennsylvania, United States of America.

In summary the family of Warren is doing well with his brother Jim working at the University of Maine with a beautiful family of four boys. They all know the story of their Uncle Warren. Very proud they are as they remember every Memorial Day, Veterans Day and especially Warrens birthday – 3 May 1948 and the day of his passing 5 December 1968.

References:
http://www.virtualwall.org/db/BreeceWW01a.htm
http://www.thewall-usa.com/info.asp?recid=5470
http://www.vvmf.org/thewall/Wall_Id_No=5494

Robert Raymond Brett
(Penndel)

United States Navy
Headquarters & Service Company, 2nd Battalion, 26th Marine Regiment, 1st Marine Division

Recipient of the Legion of Merit

Rank: Lieutenant (O-3), Reserve
Length of Service: less than 1 year

MOS: Chaplain
Born: January 3, 1936
Died: Thursday, February 22, 1968
Age: 32
Circumstances: hostile, ground casualty, artillery, rocket or mortar
Location: Khe Sanh, Quang Tri Province (I Corps Tactical Zone)
Tour Started: September 15, 1967
Length of time in Vietnam: 160 days
Parents: Margaret Brett
Marital Status: single
Religion: Roman Catholic
High School: St. Gabriel's School
College: Catholic University
Seminary: St. Mary's Manor, Penndel PA
Ordained: February 1962
Final resting place: Arlington National Cemetery
Location on The Wall: panel 40E, row 58

The Roman Catholic priest grew up on S. 29th Street in South Philadelphia, graduating from nearby St. Gabriel's School and later Catholic University in Washington DC. He was ordained in the Marist order in 1962 and enlisted in the Navy in 1967 while teaching at Immaculata Seminary in Lafayette, LA. The Navy lieutenant was killed on February 2, 1968, in Khe Sanh, Quang Tri Province, Viet Nam, at the height of the Tet offensive, when a Viet Cong mortar round hit a bunker in which he was celebrating Mass for members of the 3rd Marine Division. He was 32 years old. Brett "was neither a hawk or a dove, but he wanted to be where the men needed him most, so he requested overseas combat duty in Viet Nam," recalled a family member.

Chaplain Brett and his assistant, Marine PFC Alexander Chin died together at Khe Sanh. Chaplain Brett was originally buried in Penndel and Chin was buried in Princess Anne, Maryland. In 1998, Brett's family arranged to have him reburied on Chaplain's Hill in Arlington National Cemetery. In the spring of 1999, Chin's family agreed to have him buried with Brett at Arlington.

Brett Hall at the Naval Chaplain's School in Newport, Rhode Island was named after him.

Brett is one of the sixteen Chaplains who lost their lives in Vietnam.

References:
http://www.virtualwall.org/db/BrettRR01a.htm
http://www.thewall-usa.com/info.asp?recid=5543
http://www.vvmf.org/thewall/Wall_Id_No=5567

Donald Bruce Campbell

(Richboro)

United States Marine Corps
VMA-121, Marine Aircraft Group 12,
1st Marine Aircraft Wing

Recipient of the Air Medal

Rank: Major (O-4), Enlisted
Length of Service: 10 years
MOS: 7501, Pilot
Born: May 31, 1936
Died: Sunday, July 28, 1968
Age: 32
Circumstances: hostile, air loss or crash over land
Location: Thua Thien Province (I Corps Tactical Zone)
Tour Started:

Length of time in Vietnam:
Marital Status: single
Religion: Roman Catholic
High School: Ensley High School
College: Auburn University
Final resting place: Arlington National Cemetery
Location on The Wall: panel 50W, row 23

Donald Campbell was born May 31, 1936 in Passaic, New Jersey. He attended schools in Clifton NJ before his family moved to Alabama. He graduated from Ensley High School in 1954 and attended Auburn University for two years and then enrolled in the Naval Air Cadet Station, located in Pensacola, Florida. He enlisted in the US Marine Corps in June 1957 and began flight training the following spring. In December 1959, he was commissioned a Second Lieutenant.

He was qualified to fly to A4E Skyhawk, the C130 Hercules and also flew refueling missions as well as support early on in Vietnam.

While stationed at Chu Lai during his third tour of duty, Campbell, who now held the rank of Major, embarked on a bombing mission on July 28, 1968. His plane never returned. It was unclear whether the aircraft was hit by ground fire or failed to recover from a dive-bombing maneuver. Campbell was unable to eject and the aircraft crashed.

References:
http://www.virtualwall.org/dc/CampbellDB01a.htm
http://www.thewall-usa.com/info.asp?recid=7574
http://www.vvmf.org/thewall/Wall_Id_No=7592

John Elton Candy
(Langhorne)

United States Marine Corps
E Company, 2nd Battalion, 9th Marine Regiment,
3rd Marine Division

Rank: Private First Class (E-2),
Length of Service: 2 years
MOS: 0311, Rifleman
Born: November 15, 1947
Died: Friday, October 11, 1968
Age: 20
Circumstances: non-hostile, ground casualty, accidental grenade explosion
Location: Quang Tri Province (I Corps Tactical Zone)
Tour Started: October 3, 1968

Length of time in Vietnam: 8 days
Marital Status: single
Religion: Protestant
High School: Neshaminy High School
Final resting place: Cedar Hill Cemetery (East), Philadelphia PA
Location on The Wall: panel 41W, row 44

A friend of his from the USS Randolph remembers that Candy used to go home with him, on weekends off, to Rocky Mount, North Carolina. His friend found it amusing that Candy had never seen a hog before. Candy had two tattoos, "Mom" on one arm and "Dad" on the other. His friend recalls that Candy was also a fine singer.

He was a member of Platoon 2003 at MCRD Parris Island, SC in 1966.

References:
http://www.virtualwall.org/dc/CandyJE01a.htm
http://www.thewall-usa.com/info.asp?recid=7691
http://www.vvmf.org/thewall/Wall_Id_No=7709

Michael J. Ciesielka Jr.
(Eddington)

United States Army
A Company, 5th Battalion, 7th Cavalry Regiment,
1st Cavalry Division

Rank: 1st Lieutenant (O-2), Reserve
Length of Service: 1 year
MOS: 1542, Infantry Unit Commander
Born: January 23, 1948
Died: Monday, December 9, 1968
Age: 20
Circumstances: hostile, ground casualty, gun or small arms fire

Location: Binh Long Province (III Corps Tactical Zone)
Tour Started: November 3, 1968
Length of time in Vietnam: 36 days
Marital Status: married (Patricia)
Religion: Roman Catholic
High School: Holy Ghost Preparatory
College: Penn State University
Final resting place: Beverly National Cemetery
Location on The Wall: panel 37W, row 32

A grade school classmate remembers Ciesielka was Captain of the Safety Patrol in St. Charles Elementary School (1959-1960). Ciesielka was one of the youngest of his classmates at Holy Ghost Preparatory but is remembered as someone who took his responsibilities seriously. He was awarded the American Legion Award for leadership, courage, and scholarship. While in high school he participated in wrestling and drama. He also helped the Catholic Youth Organization get started at his church.

From the time he was a young boy, Michael had planned on making the Army his career. He believed in the Vietnam War and made his parents promise not to disclose to the Army that he had asthma – a condition that would have kept him out of the Army. Michael enlisted in the Army at the age of 19 on the day he was supposed to begin his second term at Penn State University. After completing basic and officers' training he came home for a 30 day leave before departing for Vietnam. He left the day before Thanksgiving 1968. He was in country only 9 days when he was killed on December 9, 1968 near the Cambodia border. He and his men had been airlifted by helicopter to search for the enemy. His unit was ambushed and he was hit by mortar shrapnel and killed instantly. He was 20 years old and had celebrated his first wedding anniversary just the week before.

References:
http://www.virtualwall.org/dc/CiesielkaMJ01a.htm
http://www.thewall-usa.com/info.asp?recid=9111
http://www.vvmf.org/thewall/Wall_Id_No=9127
The Sunday Intelligencer, Vol. 96, No. 126, May 27, 1984

Robert Lee Clampffer
(Hulmeville)

United States Army
B Company, 3rd Battalion, 1st Infantry Regiment,
11th Infantry Brigade, Americal Division

Rank: Corporal (E-4) (posthumous promotion), Drafted
Length of Service: less than 1 year
MOS: 11B10, Infantryman
Born: September 26, 1947
Died: Monday, May 6, 1968
Age: 20
Circumstances: hostile, ground casualty, burns
Location: Quang Ngai Province (I Corps Tactical Zone)
Tour Started: January 5, 1968
Length of time in Vietnam: 122 days
Marital Status: single
Religion: Lutheran
Final resting place: Philadelphia National Cemetery
Location on The Wall: panel 56E, row 2

References:
http://www.virtualwall.org/dc/ClampfferRL01a.htm
http://www.thewall-usa.com/info.asp?recid=9141
http://www.vvmf.org/thewall/Wall_Id_No=9157

Dennis Thomas Cunnane
(Levittown)

United States Marine Corps
M Company, 3rd Battalion, 1st Marine Regiment,
1st Marine Division

Rank: Private First Class (E-2), Enlisted
Length of Service: less than 1 year
MOS: 0311, Rifleman
Born: June 19, 1948
Died: Wednesday, January 31, 1968
Age: 19
Circumstances: hostile, ground casualty, gun or small arms fire
Location: Quang Tri Province (I Corps Tactical Zone)
Tour Started: November 14, 1967
Length of time in Vietnam: 78 days
Marital Status: single (engaged to Marsha)
Religion: Roman Catholic
High School: Neshaminy High School, class of 1967
Final resting place: Resurrection Cemetery, Cornwells Heights
Location on The Wall: panel 36E, row 4

In late 1967, 3rd Battalion, 1st Marines, and reinforcing elements formed Battalion Landing Team 3/1 embarked in the amphibious warfare ships of Task Force 76.5 [(USS Valley Forge (LPH 8), USS Navarro (APA 215), USS Alamo (LSD 33), USS Whetstone (LSD 27), and USS Vernon County (LST 1161)]. BLT 3/1 provided an amphibious and airmobile ready reserve force for the 3rd Marine Amphibious Force and found themselves heavily committed during the TET 68 offensive.

During operations ashore between 25 Jan and 08 Feb 1968, the 3/1 Marines lost at least 42 men; of these, not less than thirteen were Mike Company casualties.

A former member of Cunnane's unit remembers him:
Dennis was a happy-go-lucky guy who we all thought caught a break when he was transferred to a job in the rear. However, as we went afloat and things became very desperate with a huge shortage of men Dennis volunteered to come back out into the field when he could have stayed in the relative security of the rear battalion area. He was highly respected and regarded as one of us and put his life on the line for all of us in Mike 3/1. He was always smiling and seemed really too good of a person to be a combat Marine. He was a very good Marine and displayed his grit and determination each time we would go into battle. He was one of the nicest people any of us had ever met. Fairly reserved for a grunt marine. Something he had inside of him was envied by all who knew him. He was the type of man that you wished your daughter would someday marry.

He joined the Marine Corps just four days after his graduation from high school.

In one of his letters home, Cunnane wrote: "We are doing a job which I and a lot of others think has to be done now and not later. Ask those protesters what they have done to protect our freedom."

His mother said the family received a letter from Dennis on the same day he was killed. "We are going to hit the bush tomorrow, and will run right into VC the way I hear it. So wish me luck. I will write you after the operation and tell you what it was like."

References:
http://www.virtualwall.org/dc/CunnaneDT01a.htm
http://www.thewall-usa.com/info.asp?recid=11474
http://www.vvmf.org/thewall/Wall_Id_No=11481

Philip Anthony D'Amico Jr.
(Morrisville)

United States Marine Corps
A Company, 1st Battalion, 26th Marine Regiment,
5th Marine Division

Rank: Private First Class (E-2), Enlisted
Length of Service: less than 1 year
MOS: 0351, Antitank Assaultman
Born: January 28, 1949
Died: Sunday, August 18, 1968
Age: 19
Circumstances: hostile; ground casualty, gun or small arms fire
Location: Thua Thien Province (I Corps Tactical Zone)
Tour Started: July 27, 1968
Length of time in Vietnam: 22 days

Marital Status: single
Religion: Roman Catholic
High School: Frankford High School, Philadelphia PA
Final resting place: Holy Sepulcher Cemetery, Philadelphia PA
Location on The Wall: panel 48W, row 40

D'Amico left Frankford High School during his senior year and served four months in the Merchant Marine prior to enlisting in the Marine Corps in February 1968. He was survived by his mother, one sister and his maternal grandmother.

The 1st Bn, 13th Marines had an artillery firing position located on the Cao Dei peninsula, a thumb of land which protrudes into Cau Hai Bay about 4 kilometers northwest of Phu Loc. Just before 2 am on 18 August 1968 the firing position was taken under attack, first by mortars and then by sappers who penetrated the perimeter and caused considerable damage with satchel charges before the Marines ejected them and restored the perimeter.

Two platoons from Alpha 1/26 had been sent from their respective positions as reaction forces - and by chance intercepted the enemy force as they withdrew from the peninsula. In a night engagement, the Alpha 1/26 Marines took the VC under fire before the enemy force broke contact and disappeared into the nearby mountains. D'Amico was one of the seventeen Marines killed in these two engagements.

References:
http://www.virtualwall.org/dd/DamicoPA01a.htm
http://www.thewall-usa.com/info.asp?recid=11812
http://www.vvmf.org/thewall/Wall_Id_No=11679

113

Michael Francis Deeny III

(Levittown)

United States Army
A Company, 2nd Battalion, 502nd Infantry Regiment,
101st Airborne Division

Rank: Private First Class (E-3),
Length of Service: less than 1 year
MOS: 11B1P; Infantryman (Airborne Qualified)
Born: December 3, 1949
Died: Tuesday, May 21, 1968
Age: 18
Circumstances: hostile; ground casualty; artillery, rocket or mortar

Location: Thua Thien Province (I Corps Tactical Zone)
Tour Started: May 9, 1968
Length of time in Vietnam: 12 days
Parents: Michael and Joan Deeny
Siblings: one brother – Kevin; five sisters – Mary, Joan,
Elizabeth, Kathleen, and Alice
Marital Status: married to Patricia, one daughter – Robin Lynn
Religion: Roman Catholic
High School: Woodrow Wilson High School
Final resting place: Beverly National Cemetery
Location on The Wall: panel 64E, row 13

A friend of Deeny's from Levittown recalls that Deeny was kind
of wild and got his friends into 'weird situations' in Tullytown
and the Levittown Shopping Center.

References:
http://www.virtualwall.org/dd/DeenyMF01a.htm
http://www.thewall-usa.com/info.asp?recid=12590
http://www.vvmf.org/thewall/Wall_Id_No=12754

Paul Leslie Dennis
(Cornwells Heights)

United States Marine Corps
D Company, 1st Battalion, 1st Marine Regiment,
1st Marine Division

Rank: Lance Corporal (E-3), Enlisted
Length of Service: less than 1 year
MOS: 0331, Machine Gunner
Born: April 5, 1949
Died: Thursday, April 25, 1968

Age: 19
Circumstances: hostile; ground casualty; artillery, rocket, or mortar
Location: Quang Tri Province (I Corps Tactical Zone)
Tour Started: July 19, 1967
Length of time in Vietnam: 281 days
Parents: Mr. and Mrs. Victor Dennis
Siblings: one sister (Helen); one brother (Robert)
Marital Status: single
Religion: Roman Catholic
High School: Bensalem High School
Final resting place: Beverly National Cemetery
Location on The Wall: panel 52E, row 4

Dennis may have been sent to Vietnam on an error by the Marine Corps. His brother Robert, a Seabee, had volunteered for a second tour in Vietnam and that should have kept Paul from being sent overseas. Paul was killed when he was struck by shell fragments during fighting at Quang Tri. He had been wounded in action a month earlier and after recuperation had returned to his unit. Paul left Bensalem High School during his junior year in 1966 to enlist in the Marine Corps.

References:
http://www.virtualwall.org/dd/DennisPL01a.htm
http://www.thewall-usa.com/info.asp?recid=12911
http://www.vvmf.org/thewall/Wall_Id_No=12966

John Turner Dunlap III
(Feasterville)

United States Army
D Company, 3rd Battalion, 21st Infantry Regiment,
196th Infantry Brigade, Americal Division

Rank: 2nd Lieutenant (O-1),
Length of Service: 1 year
MOS: 1542, Infantry Unit Commander
Born: February 16, 1946
Died: April 29, 1968
Age: 22
Circumstances: hostile; ground casualty; other explosive device
Location: Thua Thien Province (I Corps Tactical Zone)
Tour Started: February 7, 1968

Length of time in Vietnam: 82 days
Parents: John and Dorothy Dunlap
Siblings: one sister (Susan)
Marital Status: single
Religion: Lutheran
High School: Neshaminy High School, class of 1964
College: Trenton Junior College and Rider College
Final resting place: Lawnview Memorial Park, Philadelphia PA
Location on The Wall: panel 53E, row 4

John worked briefly at the Rohm & Haas Chemical plant in Bristol PA where his father was a Maintenance Supervisor. His mother remembers that John never commented on the war in any of his letters home. He was more concerned about his family and the Philadelphia Phillies.

References:
http://www.virtualwall.org/dd/DunlapJT01a.htm
http://www.thewall-usa.com/info.asp?recid=14222
http://www.vvmf.org/thewall/Wall_Id_No=14227

James Walker Guest

(Levittown)

United States Army
C Battery, 1st Battalion, 30th Artillery, 41st Artillery Group,
I Field Force

Rank: Private First Class (E-3), drafted
Length of Service: less than 1 year
MOS: 13A10, Field Artillery, Basic
Born: April 7, 1946
Died: Tuesday, February 20, 1968
Age: 21
Circumstances: non-hostile; ground casualty; died of other causes, vehicle crash (killed when a truck in which he was riding overturned)
Location: Binh Dinh Province (II Corps Tactical Zone)
Tour Started: January 18, 1968
Length of time in Vietnam: 33 days
Parents: Mr. & Mrs. James Guest

Siblings: one brother (Robert); one sister (Bonnie)
Marital Status: married to Penny (Reynolds)
Religion: Methodist
High School: Pennsbury High School, class of 1964
College: Temple University
Final resting place: Beverly National Cemetery
Location on The Wall: panel 40E, row 40

The editors contacted James's former Battery Commander who wrote:

In 1968 I was the Battery Commander of Charlie Battery 1st Bn 30th Arty (155mm Towed Howitzer) 1st Cav Div on a hilltop firebase named Lz Laramie in northern II Corps Vietnam . PFC James Walker Guest arrived in country on Jan 18,1968 and was assigned to my unit several days later, just before TET. He was assigned to the ammo section.

In January the Battalion HQ, Alpha and Bravo Batteries moved north into I Corps with two Brigades of the Ist Cav. In the 2nd week of February I was alerted to prepare to move and join them. We had to airlift all the equipment off the hill to LZ English, a large LZ about 10 miles to the SE, where we joined up with our vehicles and the rest of our supply, maintenance and ammo sections. We loaded our basic load of ammo (approx. 1,000 rounds) and all of the other unit equipment on the vehicles and headed south on QL1 for the 50-60 mile road march to Qui Nhon. About halfway there one of the ammo trucks, towing a trailer, overcorrected while trying to negotiate a gradual 75 degree turn to the right. As a result the truck with soldiers aboard flipped over on the three foot embankment and flipped the soldiers into the rice paddy, followed by the pallets of projectiles and powder. James and another soldier were submerged for a while under one of the pallets, five other soldiers were injured. The soldiers at the end of the convoy reacted immediately while my driver called for Medevac. All of them were alive when we loaded them aboard the choppers.

The convoy regrouped and proceeded to Qui Nhon. I was informed later that night that James and another soldier had died

References:

http://www.virtualwall.org/dg/GuestJW01a.htm
http://www.thewall-usa.com/info.asp?recid=20370
http://www.vvmf.org/thewall/Wall_Id_No=20359

George W. Hamilton Jr.
(Warminster)

United States Army
C Company, 1st Battalion, 52nd Infantry Regiment,
198th Infantry Brigade, Americal Division

Rank: Sergeant (E-5), Drafted

Length of Service: 1 year
MOS: 11B40, Infantryman
Born: January 28, 1947
Died: Thursday, July 11, 1968
Age: 21
Circumstances: hostile; ground casualty; other explosive device
Location: Quang Ngai Province (I Corps Tactical Zone)
Tour Started: October 6, 1967
Length of time in Vietnam: 279 days
Parents:
Siblings: one brother, three sisters (Suse, Marilyn, and Phyllis)
Marital Status: married July 8, 1967
Religion: Lutheran
High School: Dobbins Vocational High School (class of 1964), Philadelphia PA
Final resting place: George Washington Memorial Park, Plymouth Meeting PA
Location on The Wall: panel 52W, row 15

Former members of Hamilton's unit remember him:

"George was my first squad leader. He was an outstanding, brave and courageous young man. He exemplified the highest standards of US Military conduct and was a strong and capable leader. I will always miss his humor and the strength of his character."

"George was a great guy. He helped me, through those first shaky weeks, until I could get my feet on the ground. A true and courageous leader, in a very difficult, dangerous and harrowing, war zone."

"I was with George on July 10, 1968. We had been on patrol for a couple of days when we hit a booby trap. What I remember was the day before, he asked me how to

spell   *anniversary.*
George was a very special person to everyone that knew him. He was always there for me and I for him, except when he needed me most. We had landed and were walking through a brushy Tactical Zone when the explosion happened. George was really tore up, but never in deep pain. I was with him the next day when he passed. He was always thinking of his wife and family. He had asked me to contact them, but as it was with most of us, I could not do it at the time."

"Ham" Hamilton played quarterback at Murrell Dobbins Vocational High School, where he studied mechanical design before graduating in 1964. He was a draftsman at Gimpel Machine Works, Inc. for two years before entering the Army in October 1966. Hamilton died in Da Nang, Quang Nam Province, when he was hit by fragments from an enemy booby trap.

References:
http://www.virtualwall.org/dh/HamiltonGW01a.htm
http://www.thewall-usa.com/info.asp?recid=20972
http://www.vvmf.org/thewall/Wall_Id_No=20958

Joseph Henry Hanks III
(Croydon)

United States Marine Corps
C Company, 1st Battalion, 5th Marine Regiment,
1st Marine Division

Rank: Lance Corporal (E-3), Enlisted
Length of Service: 2 years
MOS: 0311, Rifleman
Born: November 18, 1948
Died: Saturday, December 14, 1968
Age: 20
Circumstances: hostile; ground casualty; gun or small arms fire
Location: Quang Nam Province (I Corps Tactical Zone)

Tour Started: September 6, 1968
Length of time in Vietnam: 99 days
Parents:
Siblings: 2 brothers (Francis and John)
Marital Status: married
Religion: Protestant
Final resting place: Beverly National Cemetery
Location on The Wall: panel 36W, row 24

Joseph went through basic training with Platoon 113, C
Company, 1st Recruit Training Battalion. The training dates
were from January 12, 1966 to March 2, 1966.

References:
http://www.virtualwall.org/dh/HanksJH01a.htm
http://www.thewall-usa.com/info.asp?recid=21166
http://www.vvmf.org/thewall/Wall_Id_No=21152

Frank Elton Hilte

(Danboro)

United States Army
Headquarters & Headquarters Battery, 6th Battalion,
15th Artillery Regiment, 1st Infantry Division

Recipient of the Bronze Star with V for Valor

Rank: Staff Sergeant (E-6), Enlisted
Length of Service: 18 years
MOS: 13E40, Cannon Fire Direction Specialist
Born: April 10, 1930
Died: February 9, 1968
Age: 37
Circumstances: hostile; ground casualty; gun or small arms fire
Location: Binh Duong Province (III Corps Tactical Zone)
Tour Started: October 22, 1967
Length of time in Vietnam: 110 days
Marital Status: married, 1 son (Ken)
Religion: Protestant

Final resting place: Arlington National Cemetery
Location on The Wall: panel 38E, row 51

Frank was posthumously awarded the Bronze Star with V for Valor. The citation is as follows:

DEPARTMENT OF THE ARMY
HEADQUARTERS 1ST INFANTRY DIVISION
APO San Francisco 96345

GENERAL ORDERS 29 March 1968
NUMBER 2823

AWARD OF THE BRONZE STAR MEDAL

1. TC 320. The following AWARD is announced posthumously.

HILTE, FRANK E RA15420638 (SSAN:245 38 5654) STAFF SERGEANT E6 United States Army, Headquarters and Headquarters Battery 6th Howitzer Battalion 15th Artillery

Awarded: Bronze Start with "V" device
Date of action: 9 February 1968
Theater: Republic of Vietnam

Reason: For heroism in connection with military operations against a hostile force: On this date, Sergeant Hilte was serving as an artillery forward observer attach to an infantry unit during battalion-minus search and destroy mission. Before the friendly forces moved out, Sergeant Hilte called in artillery fire to saturate the area where enemy contact had been made earlier. As the units moved into the suspected area, they were subjected to heavy automatic weapons, rocket propelled grenades, and small arms fire by a numerically superior Viet Cong force. Without hesitation or regard for his own personal safety, Sergeant Hilte moved through the heavy enemy fire to a forward position and began calling in artillery fire onto the well camouflaged and concealed insurgent positions. He remained in a completely exposed position and directed devastating fire on the Viet Cong. His quick but accurate calculations and adjustments of artillery fire enabled the friendly forces to gain vital fire superiority and they were soon able to drive the enemy force from the area with heavy losses. As Sergeant Hilte was adjusting blocking fires on the retreating insurgents he was mortally wounded by hostile small arms fire. His dauntless courage, exemplary skill and determined efforts undoubtedly save many friendly lives and contributed significantly to the ultimate defeat of a large Viet Cong force. Staff Sergeant Hilte's outstanding display of aggressiveness, devotion to duty, and personal bravery is in keeping with the finest traditions of the military service and reflects great credit upon himself, the 1st Infantry Division, and the United States Army.

Authority: By direction of the President, under provisions of Executive Order 11046, 24 August 1962.

FOR THE COMMANDER:

ARCHIE R. HYLE
Colonel, GS
Chief of Staff

OFFICIAL:

(Signed: A. Crowley Jr., Cpt, AGC)

W.C. ALEXANDER
Captain, AGC
Assistant Adjutant General

References:
http://www.virtualwall.org/dh/HilteFE01a.htm
http://www.thewall-usa.com/info.asp?recid=23296
http://www.vvmf.org/thewall/Wall_Id_No=23276

Gary David Holland

(Quakertown)

United States Army
C Company, 2nd Battalion, 12th Infantry Regiment,
25th Infantry Division

Rank: Private First Class (E-3), Drafted
Length of Service: less than 1 year
MOS: 11C10; Indirect Fire Infantryman
Born: September 5, 1944
Died: Friday, February 9, 1968
Age: 23
Circumstances: hostile; ground casualty; multiple fragmentation wounds
Location: Binh Duong Province (III Corps Tactical Zone)
Tour Started: January 6, 1968
Length of time in Vietnam: 34 days
Parents: Synda (Bartholomew) Boehm
Siblings: 1 sister
Marital Status: single
Religion: Lutheran
High school: Palisades High School, class of 1966
Final resting place: Union Cemetery, Hellertown PA
Location on The Wall: panel 38E, row 51

A fellow platoon member of Gary's recalls that he was killed while on an LP (Listening Post) assignment along with Warren Beaumont (also from Bucks County), Rockford Everett, and Russell Cornish.

A former high school classmate recalls Gary as one of the nicest persons she ever met. She named her son Gary after him.

References:

http://www.virtualwall.org/dh/HollandGD01a.htm
http://www.thewall-usa.com/info.asp?recid=23737
http://www.vvmf.org/thewall/Wall_Id_No=23716

Theodore K Kaleikini Jr.
(Levittown)

United States Army
Detachment A-431 (CAI) (CAI), D Company,
5th Special Forces Group

Rank: Sergeant (E-5), Enlisted
Length of Service: 2 years
MOS: 05B4S, Radio Operator (Special Forces Qualified)
Born: May 31, 1945
Died: Thursday, January 18, 1968
Age: 22
Circumstances: hostile; ground casualty; multiple
fragmentation wounds
Location: Kien Phong Province (IV Corps Tactical Zone)
Tour Started: November 3, 1967
Length of time in Vietnam: 76 days
Parents: Theodore Sr. and Myra
Siblings: 2 brothers (Harris and Lani), 1 sister (Cirilla)
Marital Status: single
Religion: Mormon
High School: Woodrow Wilson High School
Final resting place: Beverly National Cemetery
Location on The Wall: panel 34E, row 69

Theodore, a member of the "Green Berets," was killed at a mountain outpost Thursday, January 18, 1968. He enlisted in August, 1965, leaving his job at the National Biscuit Co., Philadelphia, and was trained in the Army Special Forces for duty as a radio operator.

References:
http://www.virtualwall.org/dk/KaleikiniTK01a.htm
http://www.thewall-usa.com/info.asp?recid=27128
http://www.vvmf.org/thewall/Wall_Id_No=27094

John Michael Lyons
(Andalusia)

United States Army
D Company, 2nd Battalion, 506th Infantry Regiment,
101st Airborne Division

Rank: Corporal (E-4), posthumous promotion, Enlisted
Length of Service: 1 year
MOS: 11B1P, Infantryman (Airborne Qualified)
Born: January 12, 1948
Died: Monday, September 16, 1968
Age: 20
Circumstances: hostile; ground casualty; multiple fragmentation wounds
Location: Hau Nghia Province (III Corps Tactical Zone)
Tour Started: June 3, 1968
Length of time in Vietnam: 105 days
Marital Status: married to Anna, 1 son
Religion: Roman Catholic
High School: Father Judge High School, Philadelphia PA
College:
Final resting place: Resurrection Cemetery, Cornwells Heights PA
Location on The Wall: panel 43W, row 6

"I really appreciate everybody's prayers, and I pray a lot myself," Lyons wrote in his last letter from Vietnam, which arrived the day after he died. "I'll be O.K. and if anything happens to me, I'll still be O.K. God's given me a good family, a wonderful wife, and a son to be proud of. I hate this war, but while I'm in it, I'll do my best." Lyons, nicknamed "Cubby" by his family, grew up in Philadelphia and was a 1966 graduate of Father Judge High School. He was a telephone lineman for 18 months before enlisting in the Army in September, 1967. The 20-year-old corporal, a rifleman, assigned to Company D of the 2nd Battalion, 506th Infantry, 101st Airborne Division, died in Vietnam on September 16, 1968. He was survived by his wife, Anna, who is active in Vietnam veteran causes in Bucks County, a son, and his parents. John lived on Highland

Avenue, in Andalusia, Bucks County, Pennsylvania. Source: Philadelphia Daily News 10/26/1987

References:
http://www.virtualwall.org/dl/LyonsJM01a.htm
http://www.thewall-usa.com/info.asp?recid=31702
http://www.vvmf.org/thewall/Wall_Id_No=31758

Charles Carter Meyers
(Warminster)

United States Army
B Battery, 5th Battalion, 2nd Artillery, 23rd Artillery Group,
II Field Force

Rank: Private First Class (E-3), Drafted
Length of Service: less than 1 year
MOS: 13F10, Automatic Weapons Crewman
Born: December 21, 1947
Died: Saturday, August 31, 1968
Age: 20
Circumstances: non-hostile; ground casualty; accidental homicide
Location: Binh Duong Province (III Corps Tactical Zone)
Tour Started: June 12, 1968
Length of time in Vietnam: 80 days
Marital Status: single
Religion: Baptist
High School: William Tennant High School, class of 1966
Location on The Wall: panel 45W, row 15

References:
http://www.virtualwall.org/dm/MeyersCC01a.htm
http://www.thewall-usa.com/info.asp?recid=35025
http://www.vvmf.org/thewall/Wall_Id_No=33735

Phillip Daniel Miller

(Quakertown)

United States Marine Corps
L Company, 3rd Battalion, 3rd Marine Regiment,
3rd Marine Division

Rank: Lance Corporal (E-3), Enlisted
Length of Service: less than 1 year
MOS: 0311, Rifleman
Born: March 4, 1949
Died: Tuesday, May 28, 1968
Age: 19
Circumstances: hostile; ground casualty; gun or small arms fire
Location: Quang Tri Province (I Corps Tactical Zone)
Tour Started: December 14, 1967
Length of time in Vietnam: 166 days
Parents: Mr. & Mrs. George Miller
Marital Status: single
Religion: Protestant
Final resting place: St. John's Lutheran Cemetery, Spinnerstown PA
Location on The Wall: panel 64W, row 10

References:
http://www.virtualwall.org/dm/MillerPD02a.htm
http://www.thewall-usa.com/info.asp?recid=35426
http://www.vvmf.org/thewall/Wall_Id_No=34134

John Russell Millikan
(Spinnerstown)

United States Army
D Company, 2nd Battalion, 27th Infantry Regiment,
25th Infantry Division

Rank: Sergeant (E-5), Drafted
Length of Service: 1 year
MOS: 11B40, Infantryman
Born: July 23, 1947
Died: Sunday, August 18, 1968
Age: 21
Circumstances: hostile; ground casualty; gun or small arms fire
Location: Tay Ninh Province (III Corps Tactical Zone)
Tour Started: May 17, 1968
Length of time in Vietnam: 93 days

Parents: Mr. & Mrs. Robert Wetzel
Marital Status: single
Religion: Lutheran
Final resting place: St. John's Lutheran Cemetery, Spinnerstown PA
Location on The Wall: panel 48W, row 14

A high school friend remembers, *"John was a great person to many as long as you didn't do him, his family, or his friends any wrong doing. He was a strong willed type of guy who would be there for you if you needed help. He was smart, gentle, and kind. . He was my hero when he was alive and he is every ones hero now".*

References:
http://www.virtualwall.org/dm/MillikanJR01a.htm
http://www.thewall-usa.com/info.asp?recid=35512
http://www.vvmf.org/thewall/Wall_Id_No=34219

Terry Joseph Patrick Neill
(Bristol)

United States Army
D Company, 6th Battalion, 31st Infantry Regiment,
9th Infantry Division

Rank: Corporal (E-4) posthumous promotion, Enlisted
Length of Service: less than 1 year
MOS: 11B10, Infantryman
Born: October 25, 1948
Died: Sunday, June 23, 1968
Age: 19
Circumstances: non-hostile; ground casualty; accidental
homicide (accidently shot and killed in a perimeter defense
zone)

Location: Gia Dinh Province (III Corps Tactical Zone)
Tour Started: May 26, 1968
Length of time in Vietnam: 28 days
Parents: Arthur and Dorothy
Siblings: 1 brother
Marital Status: single
Religion: Roman Catholic
High School: Bristol High School
Final resting place: Beverly National Cemetery
Location on The Wall: panel 55W, row 22

His parents said the last time they heard from their son was when he called home June 19 at 3:25 A.M. from Saigon. He said he was concerned that he had not received any mail recently.

"I told him there was probably some kind of delay and he would receive a packet of mail all at the same time," said his mother, Dorothy.

References:
http://www.virtualwall.org/dn/NeillTJ01a.htm
http://www.thewall-usa.com/info.asp?recid=37502
http://www.vvmf.org/thewall/Wall_Id_No=37533

James Frank Porter
(Warrington)

United States Army
D Company, 4th Medical Battalion, 4th Infantry Division

Rank: Private First Class (E-3), Enlisted
Length of Service: less than 1 year
MOS: 91C20, Practical Nurse

Born: June 15, 1946
Died: January 31, 1968
Age: 21
Circumstances: hostile; ground casualty; artillery, rocket or mortar
Location: Quang Ngai Province (I Corps Tactical Zone)
Tour Started: January 4, 1968
Length of time in Vietnam: 27 days
Parents: Mrs. Gloria Cohen
Siblings: 4 brothers (Norman, Daniel, Jeffrey, and David)
Marital Status: single
Religion: Protestant
High School:
College: Bucks County Community College
Final resting place: Harleigh Cemetery, Camden NJ
Location on The Wall: panel 36E, row 31

James was a social worker and psychologist assigned to the 4th Medical Battalion of the 4th Infantry Division. He had been in Vietnam only three weeks when he was killed by mortar fire. "He didn't want to go to jail, but he didn't believe in the Army or war," his mother said. When he refused to carry a gun during basic training, he was transferred to Fort Sam Houston in Texas, where he was trained as a medic.

James is one of the three namesakes of Igoe Porter Wellings Park in Warrington.

References:
http://www.virtualwall.org/dp/PorterJF01a.htm
http://www.thewall-usa.com/info.asp?recid=41306
http://www.vvmf.org/thewall/Wall_Id_No=41327

Philip Henry Radecki
(Andalusia)

United States Air Force
14th Service Squadron, 14th Air Commando Wing,
7th Air Force

Rank: Airman 1st Class (E-3), Enlisted
Length of Service: 3 years
MOS: Baker and Pastry Chef
Born: April 16, 1947
Died: Tuesday, May 7, 1968
Age: 21
Circumstances: non-hostile; ground casualty; illness or injury
(vehicle crash)
Location: Khanh Hoa Province (II Corps Tactical Zone)
Tour Started: November 14, 1967
Length of time in Vietnam: 175 days
Parents: Mr. & Mrs. Henry Radecki
Siblings: one sister (Beverly)
Marital Status: single
Religion: Episcopal
High School: Bensalem High School
Location on The Wall: panel 56E, row 30

References:
http://www.virtualwall.org/dr/RadeckiPH01a.htm
http://www.thewall-usa.com/info.asp?recid=42118
http://www.vvmf.org/thewall/Wall_Id_No=42134

142

M Raymond Reeves
(Bristol)

United States Army
C Company, 228th Assault Support Helicopter Battalion,
11th Aviation Group. 1st Cavalry Division

Rank: Specialist 4th Class (E-4), Enlisted
Length of Service: 2 years
MOS: 11H20, Infantry Direct Fire Crewman
Born: August 12, 1948
Died: Sunday, March 3, 1968
Age: 19
Circumstances: hostile; ground casualty; gun or small arms
fire
Location: Quang Tri Province
Tour Started: October 28, 1967
Length of time in Vietnam: 127 days
Marital Status: single
Religion: Baptist
High School: Delhaas High School
Final resting place: Beverly National Cemetery
Location on The Wall: panel 42E, row 56

A former member of Reeves' unit, Mel "Tex" Chappell
remembers him:

*It seems there are certain people who have touched us in the
past who live on inside us even after so many years have
passed us by. That is the way Reeves' infectious laugh and
keen sense of humor have followed me all these years. I tell
my students about him and his laugh periodically. Reeves'
favorite saying was, "Don't get me wrong soldier, check your
own self out." Then, he would laugh and so would we.*

*You could hear him coming from yards away and were glad of
it, too. Everyone wanted to be around him. He made the harsh*
143

reality of war just a little more pleasant. That is a gift to be coveted. Well, Reeves, it's been a while since Charlie Company. That was in '68. You were the first one of the boys we said good-bye to.

Reeves was a gunner and was riding left gun. He died when the CH-47, on which he was riding, took multiple hits. Charlie took a long shot and hit the airplane at high altitude and stole a wonderful person's life. That bullet took a wonderful soul from us that day. Reeves was a Christian, so he gained so much more than he had had with us, but we lost a lot when he was stolen away. I'll see you again one day. I sure hope the rest of our boys join us. I've heard some have.

References:
http://www.virtualwall.org/dr/ReevesMR01a.htm
http://www.thewall-usa.com/info.asp?recid=42766
http://www.vvmf.org/thewall/Wall_Id_No=42780

Gary Paul Rowlett

(Feasterville)

United States Marine Corps
B Company, 1st Battalion, 3rd Marine Regiment,
3rd Marine Division

Rank: Private First Class (E-2), Enlisted
Length of Service: less than 1 year
MOS: 0311, Rifleman
Born: November 18, 1949
Died: Wednesday, July 17, 1968 (incident date – April 30, 1968)
Age: 18

Circumstances: hostile; ground casualty; artillery, rocket, or mortar
Location: Quang Tri Province (I Corps Tactical Zone)
Tour Started: April 30, 1968
Length of time in Vietnam: 78 days
Parents: Mr. & Mrs. James M. Rowlett
Siblings: two brothers and three sisters
Marital Status: single
Religion: Roman Catholic
High School: Neshaminy High School
Final resting place: Beverly National Cemetery
Location on The Wall: panel 52W, row 46

Gary was a machine gunner. He was wounded by mortar fire on April 30, 1968. He was transferred to a hospital in Yokohama, Japan, where he called his parents in early July and told them he expected to be sent home in eight days. His condition worsened, however, and he died of a kidney complication on July 17, 1968.

References:
http://www.virtualwall.org/dr/RowlettGP01a.htm
http://www.thewall-usa.com/info.asp?recid=44679
http://www.vvmf.org/thewall/Wall_Id_No=44689

Christopher Joseph Schramm
(Fairless Hills)

United States Army
Unit: 371st Radio Research Company, 509th ASA Group,
1st Cavalry Division

Rank: Specialist 4th Class (E-4), Enlisted
Length of Service: 2 years
MOS: 05D20, EW/SIGINT Identifier
Born: October 10, 1946
Died: May 13, 1968
Age: 21
Circumstances: hostile; ground casualty; other explosive
device
Location: Thua Thien Province (I Corps Tactical Zone)
Tour Started: October 10, 1967
Length of time in Vietnam: 216 days
Parents: Mr. & Mrs. John J. Schramm
Siblings: three brothers (John, Robert, and Thomas); four
sisters (Maryann, Eugenia, Dorothy, and Betty Ann)
Marital Status: single

Religion: Roman Catholic
High School: Bishop Egan High School, class of 1965
Final resting place: Resurrection Cemetery, Cornwells Heights PA
Location on The Wall: panel 60E, row 1

While en route to Camp Evans (NW of Hue), Christopher's convoy encountered land mines. When he jumped from his truck to go to the aid of his fellow soldiers, Christopher detonated the mine which took his life. He was killed two days before he was to have gone on a seven day leave to Taiwan, his first leave in 19 months.

Christopher enlisted in the Army in October 1965, after graduation from high school and a short stint in a Catholic seminary. He was originally stationed in Taiwan but when his command asked for volunteers to go to Vietnam, he was the first to step forward. He did this "because I owed it to my family ... my country to do what I can to make this a better world."

He told his parents, who had not seen him since November 1966, "I volunteered for Vietnam because there's a job to be done." He had also told one of his sisters that he did not expect to come home.

References:

http://www.virtualwall.org/ds/SchrammCJ01a.htm
http://www.thewall-usa.com/info.asp?recid=46109
http://www.vvmf.org/thewall/Wall_Id_No=46115

Leonard F. Skoniecki Jr.

(Gardenville)

United States Marine Corps
Unit: Headquarters & Maintenance Squadron-39,
Marine Aircraft Group 39, 1st Marine Aircraft Wing

Rank: Sergeant (E-5), Enlisted
Length of Service: 3 years
MOS: 0441, Logistics Man
Born: November 6, 1947
Died: September 21, 1968
Age: 20
Circumstances: hostile; air loss or crash over land
Location: Quang Tri Province (I Corps Tactical Zone)

Tour Started: June 30, 1967
Length of time in Vietnam: 449 days
Marital Status: single
Religion: Roman Catholic
Final resting place: Holy Trinity Cemetery, Nanticoke PA
Location on The Wall: panel 43W, row 57

Leonard was one of the gunners aboard CH-46D 152557
which was on a resupply mission in support of Operation
Lancaster II when it was hit by a rocket propelled grenade and
crashed in a valley north-east of the Rockpile. All members of
the crew died upon impact.

Editor's note: Operation Lancaster II was a search and clear
operation that took place in the Ca Lu area in Quang Tri
Province. Involved were elements of the 2nd and 3rd Battalions
of the 9th Marine Regiment. The operation lasted from
January 21, 1968 to November 23, 1968.

References:
http://www.virtualwall.org/ds/SkonieckiLF01a.htm
http://www.thewall-usa.com/info.asp?recid=47861
http://www.vvmf.org/thewall/Wall_Id_No=47856

Reginald Alfonso Stancil
(Bristol)

United States Army
A Battery, 2nd Battalion, 77th Artillery,
25th Infantry Division

Rank: 1st Lieutenant (O-2), Reserve
Length of Service: 2 years
MOS: 1193, Field Artillery Unit Commander
Born: May 23, 1943
Died: Friday, January 26, 1968
Age: 24
Circumstances: hostile; ground casualty; artillery, rocket or mortar
Location: Tay Ninh Province (III Corps Tactical Zone)
Tour Started: September 22, 1967
Length of time in Vietnam: 126 days
Parents: Mr. & Mrs. William Stancil
Siblings: 4 brothers (George, Lee, Joseph, and William Jr.); 4 sisters (Betty, Valerie, Jane, and Evelyn)

Marital Status: married to Elaine (Richardson)
Religion: Baptist
College: Lincoln University
Final resting place: Gettysburg National Cemetery
Location on The Wall: panel 35E, row 42

References:
http://www.virtualwall.org/ds/StancilRA01a.htm
http://www.thewall-usa.com/info.asp?recid=49408
http://www.vvmf.org/thewall/Wall_Id_No=49402

Stanley R. Stellmach Jr.
(Levittown)

United States Army
116th Assault Helicopter Company, 169th Aviation Battalion,
12th Aviation Group, 1st Aviation Brigade

Recipient of the Air Medal

Rank: Sergeant (E-5) (posthumous promotion), Enlisted
Length of Service: 1 year
MOS: 11B2F, Infantryman (Flight)
Born: October 18, 1948
Died: Sunday, April 14, 1968
Age: 19
Circumstances: non-hostile; air loss or crash over land
Location: Tay Ninh Province (III Corps Tactical Zone)
Tour Started: February 12, 1967
Length of time in Vietnam: 427 days
Parents: Mr. & Mrs. Stanley Sr.
Siblings: 1 brother (James), 7 sisters (Martha, Maryann,
Elizabeth, Irene, Ann, Florence, and Geraldine)
Marital Status: single

Religion: Roman Catholic
High School: Woodrow Wilson High School
Final resting place: Beverly National Cemetery
Location on The Wall: panel 50E, row 1

Stanley was a door gunner and the only casualty when UH-1D tail number 65-10040 suffered a tail rotor failure immediately after lifting off from a refueling pad.

Stanley is remembered by his friends as having a great smile and sense of humor. He had a wonderful spirit and was full of life. He was a great fun-loving man who extended his tour of duty in order to get an early out.

References:
http://www.virtualwall.org/ds/StellmachSR01a.htm
http://www.thewall-usa.com/info.asp?recid=49683
http://www.vvmf.org/thewall/Wall_Id_No=49674

Clifford Dale VanArtsdalen

(Perkasie)

United States Army
Unit: D Company, 1st Battalion, 20th Infantry Regiment,
11th Light Infantry Brigade, Americal Division

Rank: Specialist 4th Class (E-4), Enlisted
Length of Service: 1 year
MOS: 11C20, Indirect Fire Infantryman
Born: December 25, 1949
Died: Thursday, May 9, 1968
Age: 18
Circumstances: hostile; ground casualty; multiple
fragmentation wounds
Location: Quang Tin Province (I Corps Tactical Zone)
Tour Started: unknown
Length of time in Vietnam: unknown
Parents: Mr. & Mrs. William J.
Siblings: 4 brothers and 4 sisters
Marital Status: single
Religion: Protestant
High School: Pennridge High School
Final resting place: Gettysburg National Cemetery
Location on The Wall: panel 58E, row 1

Clifford was the youngest of ten children. He left high school before graduating and worked at a Sellersville sweater factory with his mother. He joined the Army in April 1967 after two of his friends were killed in Vietnam. He wanted to avenge their deaths.

Clifford was on a combat operation with his unit in Quang Tin Province, South Vietnam on May 9, 1968. The unit was operating about 20 miles west of the city of Tam Ky. At 1300 hours, the weapons platoon assumed a front-firing position, and Van Artsdalen and two others were sent to a position to provide a base of fire. At that time, the enemy returned a heavy volume of fire and an explosion was seen from their position. The weapons platoon sergeant near the position saw that Van Artsdalen had been hit. Two men who attempted to recover his body were also wounded. Because of heavy fire, Van Artsdalen's remains could not be recovered. Searches of the battle area were conducted as well as could be in view of the hostility in the area. Clifford Van Artsdalen is still listed among those unaccounted for in Vietnam. His official status is that of Killed In Action, Body Not Recovered.

References:
http://www.virtualwall.org/dv/VanartsdalenCD01a.htm
http://www.thewall-usa.com/info.asp?recid=53283
http://www.vvmf.org/thewall/Wall_Id_No=53255
The Sunday Intelligencer, Vol. 96, No. 126, May 27, 1984

Ronald Lee Weaver
(Quakertown)

United States Army
543rd Transportation Company, 6th Transportation Battalion,
48th Transportation Group, Army Support Command Saigon,
1st Logistics Command

Rank: Private First Class (E-3), Drafted
Length of Service: less than 1 year
MOS: 64A10, Light Vehicle Driver
Born: May 9, 1946
Died: Friday, February 23, 1968
Age: 21

Circumstances: hostile; ground casualty; artillery, rocket, or mortar
Location: Hau Nghia Province (III Corps Tactical Zone)
Tour Started: February 8, 1968
Length of time in Vietnam: 15 days
Marital Status: married
Religion: Roman Catholic
Final resting place: St. John the Baptist Cemetery, Haycock Run PA
Location on The Wall: panel 41E, row 5

References:
http://www.virtualwall.org/dw/WeaverRL01a.htm
http://www.thewall-usa.com/info.asp?recid=54938
http://www.vvmf.org/thewall/Wall_Id_No=54899

Neil William Weintraub

(Cornwells Heights)

United States Marine Corps
G Company, 2nd Battalion, 4th Marine Regiment,
3rd Marine Division

Rank: Private First Class (E-2), Enlisted
Length of Service: less than 1 year
MOS: 0341, Mortarman
Born: December 26, 1949
Died: Saturday, June 22, 1968
Age: 18
Circumstances: hostile; ground casualty; mortar attack

Location: Quang Tri Province (I Corps Tactical Zone) (Hill 512, near Khe Sanh)
Tour Started: May 8, 1968
Length of time in Vietnam: 45 days
Parents: Arthur and Kay (DiStefano)
Siblings: 2 brothers (Dominick and David); 2 sisters (Susan and Kathleen)
Marital Status: single
Religion: Roman Catholic
High School: Bensalem High School
Final resting place: Our Lady of Grace Cemetery, Langhorne PA
Location on The Wall: panel 55W, row 19

A PA Turnpike bridge in Bensalem was named after him.
He was a defensive end on the Bensalem High School football team in 1966.

References:
http://www.virtualwall.org/dw/WeintraubNW01a.htm
http://www.thewall-usa.com/info.asp?recid=55119
http://www.vvmf.org/thewall/Wall_Id_No=55079

Larry Lee York

(Trumbauersville)

United States Army
B Company, 1st Battalion, 6th Infantry Regiment,
198th Light Infantry Brigade, Americal Division

Recipient of the Bronze Star

Rank: Corporal (E-4) posthumous promotion, Drafted
Length of Service: less than 1 year
MOS: 11B10, Infantryman
Born: December 16, 1947
Died: Saturday, June 1, 1968
Age: 20
Circumstances: hostile; ground casualty; artillery, rocket, or mortar
Location: Quang Tin Province (I Corps Tactical Zone)
Tour Started: November 12, 1967
Length of time in Vietnam: 202 days
Parents: Irving Rapp and Myrtle (Rodenberger) York
Siblings: 2 brothers (Harvey and Raymond); 2 sisters (Mrs. Douglas Amey and Mary)
Marital Status: single
Religion: Reformed
High School: Quakertown High School
Location on The Wall: panel 61W row 9

References:
http://www.virtualwall.org/dy/YorkLL01a.htm
http://www.thewall-usa.com/info.asp?recid=57843
http://www.vvmf.org/thewall/Wall_Id_No=57793

1969

Dennis Michael Adams
(Andalusia)

United States Army
C Troop, 3rd Squadron, 17th Cavalry Regiment,
1st Aviation Brigade

Rank: Private First Class (E-3), Enlisted
Length of Service: 4 years
MOS: 67A1F, Aircraft Maintenance Apprentice (Flight Qualified)
Born: August 15, 1947
Died: Friday, February 28, 1969
Age: 21
Circumstances: non-hostile; ground casualty; illness or injury; vehicle loss or crash
Location: Dinh Tuong Province (IV Corps Tactical Zone)
Tour Started: September 3, 1968
Length of time in Vietnam: 178 days
Marital Status: single
Religion: Baptist
Final resting place: Beverly National Cemetery
Location on The Wall: panel 31W, row 87

References:
http://www.virtualwall.org/da/AdamsDM02a.htm
http://www.thewall-usa.com/info.asp?recid=167
http://www.vvmf.org/thewall/Wall_Id_No=209

Lee Fulton Clickner

(Bristol)

United States Army
Unit: Recon Platoon, E Company, 1st Battalion,
52nd Infantry Regiment, 198th Infantry Brigade,
Americal Division

Rank: 1st Lieutenant (O-2) posthumous promotion, Reserve
Length of Service: 2 years
MOS: 1542, Infantry Unit Commander
Born: May 18, 1945
Died: Saturday, October 25, 1969
Age: 24
Circumstances: hostile; ground casualty; gun or small arms fire
Location: Quang Ngai Province (I Corps Tactical Zone)
Tour Started: June 14, 1969
Length of time in Vietnam: 133 days
Parents: Catherine Reinheimer
Marital Status: married
Religion: Methodist
Final resting place: Gettysburg National Cemetery
Location on The Wall: panel 17W, row 116

A former member of his unit recalls Lee:

I was one, of two point men, for the recon unit Lt., Clicker commanded. The first time I met him I knew he was a man with character. He said he was going to teach me to stay alive in Nam. He saw how, afraid I was when I first arrived and on the day of his body death he saw that again. The last thing he said to me was, I'll take over point drop back to wherever you would like. This man was a true hero.

A former high school friend also remembers Lee:

Lee was a great guy, kind and funny. He enjoyed laughing. He was athletic and smart. Lee and a bunch of us guys hung out and fooled around like lots of school-age friends, cracking jokes and assuming life would be good and go on forever. It didn't for Lee. He was a terrific guy and a good friend.

References:
http://www.virtualwall.org/dc/ClicknerLF01a.htm
http://www.thewall-usa.com/info.asp?recid=9462
http://www.vvmf.org/thewall/Wall_Id_No=9478

Terrence Charles Connolly
(Levittown)

United States Army
C Company, 227th Assault Helicopter Battalion,
11th Aviation Group, 1st Cavalry Division

Rank: Corporal (E-4), Enlisted
Length of Service: 6 years
MOS: 67A1F, Aircraft Maintenance Apprentice (Flight Qualified)
Born: July 26, 1943
Died: Tuesday, October 28, 1969
Age: 26
Circumstances: non-hostile; died of other causes; air loss or crash over land
Location: Phuoc Long Province (III Corps Tactical Zone)
Tour Started: July 27, 1969
Length of time in Vietnam: 93 days
Parents: Mr. & Mrs. William

Siblings: 2 brothers (Michael and Brian), 2 sisters (Kathleen and Patricia)
Marital Status: single
Religion: Roman Catholic
Location on The Wall: panel 17W, row 126

Terrence was a helicopter observer with the First Air Cavalry Division. He re-enlisted three months before after six years of service and volunteered to return to Vietnam immediately. His father, William, said he had visited his brother, PFC. Michael Connolly, in Germany and volunteered for combat to spare his brother assignment to Vietnam. He had written to his parents that his second tour of duty "was a lot easier in comparison to the first," but his father was convinced he was "lying a little" so they would not be worried.

References:
http://www.virtualwall.org/dc/ConnollyTC01a.htm
http://www.thewall-usa.com/info.asp?recid=10143
http://www.vvmf.org/thewall/Wall_Id_No=10155

Arthur Michael Day
(Levittown)

United States Army
D Company, 4th Battalion, 47th Infantry Regiment,
9th Infantry Division

Rank: Specialist 5th Class (E-5), Enlisted
Length of Service: 1 year
MOS: 11B20, Infantryman
Born: July 18, 1948
Died: Thursday, May 8, 1969

Age: 20
Circumstances: hostile; ground casualty; other explosive
device
Location: Kien Hoa Province (IV Corps Tactical Zone)
Tour Started: November 27, 1968
Length of time in Vietnam: 162 days
Marital Status: single
Religion: Roman Catholic
Final resting place: Jefferson Barracks National Cemetery
Location on The Wall: panel 25W, row 22

A former squad mate of Arthur's remembers him:

I served with Art, in a rifle squad, during his entire time, in Vietnam. There were three of us, who spent most of our time together, including Gordon Gipner, who was killed 2/26/69. We were all we had during that awful time. I remember Art showing me a picture of his little sister. He was very proud of her. One night, he woke me and said he had a premonition of his death. I told him to go back to sleep, as it was only a dream. Little did I know. I was not with him when he died, but a piece of me died with him.

References:
http://www.virtualwall.org/dd/DayAM01a.htm
http://www.thewall-usa.com/info.asp?recid=12421
http://www.vvmf.org/thewall/Wall_Id_No=12429

Lawrence DeMilio

(Levittown)

United States Marine Corps
M Company, 3rd Battalion, 3rd Marine Regiment,
3rd Marine Division

Rank: Private First Class (E-2), Enlisted
Length of Service: less than 1 year
MOS: 0311, Rifleman
Born: August 11, 1950
Died: Saturday, May 17, 1969
Age: 18
Circumstances: non-hostile; ground casualty; died of other causes (undefined)
Location: Quang Tri Province (I Corps Tactical Zone)
Tour Started: May 13, 1969
Length of time in Vietnam: 4 days
Marital Status: single
Religion: Roman Catholic
Location on The Wall: panel 24W, row 29

References:
http://www.virtualwall.org/dd/DemilioLx01a.htm
http://www.thewall-usa.com/info.asp?recid=12840
http://www.vvmf.org/thewall/Wall_Id_No=12587

Donald Lyle Elliott
(Doylestown)

United States Marine Corps
Headquarters & Service Company, 2nd Battalion,
3rd Marine Regiment, 3rd Marine Division

Rank: Private First Class (E-2), Enlisted
Length of Service: less than 1 year
MOS: 0341, Mortarman
Born: August 7, 1950
Died: Sunday, August 10, 1969
Age: 19
Circumstances: hostile; ground casualty; artillery, rocket, or mortar
Location: Quang Tri Province, near Vandegrift Combat Base (I Corps Tactical Zone)
Tour Started: June 6, 1969

166

Length of time in Vietnam: 65 days
Parents: James and Catherine
Siblings: 1 sister (Catherine)
Marital Status: single
Religion: Protestant
Final resting place: Highland Memorial Park, Johnston RI
Location on The Wall: panel 20W, row 122

After completing high school, Donald was accepted at Western New England College in Springfield, Massachusetts. He couldn't decide between studying Architecture or Mechanical Engineering so he decided instead to enlist in the Marine Corps. He believed he would be drafted so on the day after he turned 18 he enlisted. After serving about a year, he was sent to Quang Tri Province. He was killed on August 19, 1969 just 3 days after his 19th birthday. He was serving with his unit's mortar crew when he was wounded in the back and killed instantly when his unit came under a severe barrage of rockets and grenades.

Donald was a motorcycle enthusiast who planned to attend college and study mechanical engineering after his discharge from the Marines.

References:
http://www.virtualwall.org/de/ElliottDL01a.htm
http://www.thewall-usa.com/info.asp?recid=14883
http://www.vvmf.org/thewall/Wall_Id_No=14884
The Sunday Intelligencer, Vol. 96, No. 126, May 27, 1984

Donald William Hallow
(Bristol)

United States Army
Headquarters & Headquarters Company, 2nd Battalion,
27th Infantry Regiment, 25th Infantry Division

Rank: Specialist 5th Class (E-5), Drafted
Length of Service: less than 1 year
MOS: 91B20, Medical NCO
Born: December 22, 1948
Died: Sunday, February 23, 1969
Age: 20
Circumstances: hostile; ground casualty; gun or small arms fire
Location: Tay Ninh Province (III Corps Tactical Zone)
Tour Started: September 5, 1968
Length of time in Vietnam: 171 days
Marital Status: married to Pam
Religion: Episcopal

Final resting place: Glenwood Memorial Gardens, Broomall PA

Location on The Wall: panel 31W, row 2

References:
http://www.virtualwall.org/dh/HallowDW01a.htm
http://www.thewall-usa.com/info.asp?recid=20899
http://www.vvmf.org/thewall/Wall_Id_No=20885

David William Hawryshko
(Bristol)

United States Navy
LCU-1500, NAVSUPACT Danang, Assault Craft Unit 1

Rank: Petty Officer 2nd Class (E-4), Enlisted
Length of Service: 2 years
MOS: Radioman
Born: June 8, 1948
Died: Thursday, February 27, 1969
Age: 20
Circumstances: hostile; ground casualty; artillery, rocket, or mortar
Location: Quang Nam Province (I Corps Tactical Zone)
Tour Started: May 1, 1968
Length of time in Vietnam: 302 days
Marital Status: single
Religion: Protestant
Final resting place: Fern Knoll Burial Park, Dallas TX
Location on The Wall: panel 31W, row 80

A friend of David's remembers him:

Dave was one of the proudest, most patriotic people I had the pleasure and honor of knowing while in high school. He was one of the few demanding the Pledge of Allegiance before Audio-Visual Club, or any other club meetings. His faith in our country and the need to be in Vietnam was unshakeable. I wish I had been older and known him better. I looked up to him then, and keep a special place for him in my prayers and heart still.

References:
http://www.virtualwall.org/dh/HawryshkoDW01a.htm
http://www.thewall-usa.com/info.asp?recid=22071
http://www.vvmf.org/thewall/Wall_Id_No=22054

George Raymond Huntzinger
(Langhorne)

United States Army
D Company, 1st Battalion, 52nd Infantry Regiment,
198th Infantry Brigade, Americal Division

Rank: Private First Class (E-3), Enlisted
Length of Service: less than 1 year
MOS: 11B10, Infantryman
Born: July 5, 1949
Died: Wednesday, October 29, 1969
Age: 20
Circumstances: non-hostile; ground casualty; accidental self-destruction (claymore was accidently set off)
Location: Quang Ngai Province (I Corps Tactical Zone)
Tour Started: September 11, 1969
Length of time in Vietnam: 48 days

Parents: George and Dorothy (Capelli)
Siblings: 2 brothers (Michael and Thomas)
Marital Status: single
Religion: Roman Catholic
High School: Neshaminy High School, class of 1967
Final resting place: Our Lady of Grace, Langhorne PA
Location on The Wall: panel 16W, row 2

In a letter to his parents a few weeks before he died, George said, "After I get home, if nothing else, I will have learned to appreciate life and how good I have it." He was killed about 30 miles south of Chu Lai province when a land mine he was dismantling exploded, His parents said his one big wish was that his brother Michael would not have to go to Vietnam. In his last letter home, Huntzinger said, "It's funny how you take things for granted at home." He said he never realized how much he would miss certain things until they weren't there anymore.

References:
http://www.virtualwall.org/dh/HuntzingerGR01a.htm
http://www.thewall-usa.com/info.asp?recid=24857
http://www.vvmf.org/thewall/Wall_Id_No=24832

Frederick Robert Kutzer
(Croydon)

United States Air Force
83rd Civil Engineering Squadron, 3rd Tactical Fighter Wing, 7th Air Force

Rank: Sergeant (E-4), Enlisted
Length of Service: 8 years

Born: April 23, 1941
Died: Wednesday, March 26, 1969
Age: 27
Circumstances: non-hostile; ground casualty; died of illness or injury
Location: Bien Hoa Province (III Corps Tactical Zone)
Tour Started: September 3, 1968
Length of time in Vietnam: 204 days
Marital Status: married
Religion: Lutheran
Final resting place: Beverly National Cemetery
Location on The Wall: panel 28W, row 47

References:
http://www.virtualwall.org/dk/KutzerFR01a.htm
http://www.thewall-usa.com/info.asp?recid=29110
http://www.vvmf.org/thewall/Wall_Id_No=29072

Paul Richard Lavezzoli
(Levittown)

United States Army
3rd Platoon, C Company, 2nd Battalion, 12th Cavalry Regiment,
1st Cavalry Division

Rank: 1st Lieutenant (O-2), Reserve
Length of Service: less than 1 year
MOS: 1542, Infantry Unit Commander
Born: March 26, 1944
Died: Tuesday, November 25, 1969
Age: 25
Circumstances: hostile; ground casualty; gun or small arms fire
Location: Phuoc Long Province (III Corps Tactical Zone)

Tour Started: September 24, 1969
Length of time in Vietnam: 62 days
Marital Status: single
Religion: Roman Catholic
College: University of Florida
Final resting place: Lauderdale Memorial Park, Fort Lauderdale FL
Location on The Wall: panel 16W, row 121

References:
http://www.virtualwall.org/dl/LavezzoliPR01a.htm
http://www.thewall-usa.com/info.asp?recid=29791
http://www.vvmf.org/thewall/Wall_Id_No=29855

William Herbert McDonnell
(Newtown)

United States Army
170th Assault Helicopter Company, 52nd Aviation Battalion,
17th Aviation Group, 1st Aviation Brigade

Recipient of the Air Medal

Rank: Warrant Officer (W-1),
Length of Service: 1 year
MOS: O62B, Helicopter Pilot, Utility and Light Cargo Single Rotor
Born: March 16, 1949
Died: Friday, January 24, 1969
Age: 19
Circumstances: hostile; air loss or crash over land; shot down by hostile fire
Location: Pleiku Province (II Corps Tactical Zone)
Tour Started: August 27, 1968
Length of time in Vietnam: 150 days
Parents: William & Edith
Siblings: 2 brothers (Brian and Craig), 1 sister (Patricia)
Marital Status: single
Religion: Episcopal
High School: Council Rock High School, class of 1967
Final resting place: Newtown Cemetery, Newtown PA
Location on The Wall: panel 34W, row 71

William's father said his son wrote of feeling that the United States was "right in what it's doing here," and that he frequently worked with the Army Special Forces (Green Berets) in the Central Highlands.

References:
http://www.virtualwall.org/dm/McdonnellWH01a.htm
http://www.thewall-usa.com/info.asp?recid=33776
http://www.vvmf.org/thewall/Wall_Id_No=36551

Laurence Thomas McDowell

(Levittown)

United States Army
1st Platoon, B Company, 2nd Battalion, 7th Cavalry Regiment, 1st Cavalry Division

Rank: Corporal (E-4) posthumous promotion, Enlisted
Length of Service: less than 1 year
MOS: 11B10, Infantryman
Born: June 21, 1950
Died: Monday, September 29, 1969
Age: 19
Circumstances: hostile; ground casualty; other causes (undefined)
Location: Tay Ninh Province (III Corps Tactical Zone)
Tour Started: August 24, 1969
Length of time in Vietnam: 36 days
Parents: Mr. & Mrs. John W.
Siblings: 5 brothers (Paul, John, Edwin, David and Joseph), 1 sister (Mary Jane)
Marital Status: single
Religion: Roman Catholic
High School: Bishop Egan High School
Final resting place: Resurrection Cemetery, Cornwells Heights PA
Location on The Wall: panel 17W, row 19

Laurence volunteered to go to Vietnam to join "buddies" with whom he enlisted. He was killed while on a search and destroy mission. He was struck by enemy fire during maneuvers in the Tay Ninh Province, 60 miles northwest of Saigon. He had recently written a letter to his parents and told them he had met a buddy from Levittown, with whom he had gone through basic training at Fort Benning, Ga. "I'll be home

August. Don't worry about me," he said in the letter.
A graduate of Bishop Egan High School, Fairless Hills,
Laurence planned to enter college when discharged. His
brother Paul was, at the time, a senior at West Point.

A couple of high school classmates posted remembrances
about Laurence:

*In the hallway you always stopped to say hello. you didn't have
to; you were just being kind to someone who wanted and
needed to be noticed. small talk mostly, but welcomed and
looked forward to nonetheless. always that carefree smile and
occasionally those wild burnt orange suede shoes.*

*Learning, even many years later, of your being taken brings
memories of a fine man with such a cheerful good heart. A
classmate whose courage moved him to avoid the whims of
the group and allowed him to show kindness when others did
not.*
*And, yes, those suede shoes, truly distinctive of your
individual, unique, and independent soul.*

References:
http://www.virtualwall.org/dm/McdowellLT01a.htm
http://www.thewall-usa.com/info.asp?recid=33796
http://www.vvmf.org/thewall/Wall_Id_No=36569

Michael Brian McGinniss
(Levittown)

United States Marine Corps
3rd Engineering Battalion, 3rd Marine Division

Rank: Private First Class (E-2), Enlisted
Length of Service: less than 1 year
MOS: 1371, Combat Engineer
Born: August 11, 1949
Died: Wednesday, September 17, 1969
Age: 20
Circumstances: hostile; ground casualty; other explosive device
Location: Quang Tri Province (I Corps Tactical Zone)
Tour Started: April 17, 1969
Length of time in Vietnam: 153 days
Parents: Mr. & Mrs. Joseph W. Sr.
Siblings: 2 brothers (Joseph Jr. and Robert), 4 sisters (Mary Ann, Adrienne, Coreen, and Peggy)
Marital Status: single

Religion: Roman Catholic
High School: Pennsbury High School, class of 1968
Final resting place: Resurrection Cemetery, Cornwells Heights PA
Location on The Wall: panel 18W, row 104

Michael had wanted to be a Marine since he was six. Hel was a team leader in a combat demolition platoon. He was killed by a grenade. He had wanted to be a Marine since the age of six. Michael's unit (3rd Engineering Battalion) was to be part of the 3rd Marine Division's withdrawal from Vietnam by December 15, 1969. He had been scheduled to go on leave the week after he was killed. His younger sisters received his last letter on the day he was killed. In the letter he asked them to get his room and car ready. Michael was a tackle on the Pennsbury High School football team. He was graduated in 1968. His father was a veteran of World War II and served in the Navy.

During the summer of 1969 the North Vietnamese Army made repeated attempts to drive Allied forces from the heights of Mutter's Ridge, which formed a portion of the southern boundary of the DMZ. On 17 Sep 1969, with Lima Company, 3/3 Marines, taking a real beating on Mutter's Ridge the 3rd Marine Division reinforced them with the designated rapid deployment force, India Company 3/4 Marines. Twenty-five Marines and Navy Corpsmen died in the fighting that day and the next.

Michael McGinnis, a combat engineer from the 3rd Engineer Battalion, was attached to Lima 3/3, and was one of the Marines killed during the initial fighting on 17 September.

A close friend of his posted this remembrance:

Michael was a strong young man physically but a wise, older man in his mind. He took care of his country and even his parents in the way he planned for them to be told in the event that something happened to him (as it tragically did). He was a

179

hard worker and had a great wry sense of humor. He has always been missed by those who knew him.

References:
http://www.virtualwall.org/dm/McginnisMB01a.htm
http://www.thewall-usa.com/info.asp?recid=33946
http://www.vvmf.org/thewall/Wall_Id_No=36721

Michael Anthony Pastorino
(Southampton)

United States Army
2nd Platoon, A Company, 1st Battalion, 12th Infantry Regiment,
4th Infantry Division

Rank: Specialist 4th Class (E-4), Drafted
Length of Service: less than 1 year
MOS: 11B20, Infantryman
Born: April 23, 1949

Died: Monday, November 17, 1969
Age: 20
Circumstances: hostile; ground casualty; gun or small arms fire
Location: Binh Dinh Province (II Corps Tactical Zone)
Tour Started: June 9, 1969
Length of time in Vietnam: 161 days
Parents: Daniel and Catherine
Siblings: 5 brothers (David, Peter, Jerry, Jeffrey, and Christopher)
Marital Status: single (engaged to Helen)
Religion: Roman Catholic
High School: Bishop McDevitt High School
Final resting place: Beverly National Cemetery
Location on The Wall: panel 16W, row 89

Michael was a Green Beret who "never complained about the war". He was killed in action in Vietnam during a combat patrol.

He was one of five sons of a Southampton shoe repairman and a homemaker His parents said he never had complained about his duties in his letters and had told them the Army "is what you make it - it can be tough or easy, depending on yourself." Michael left Bishop McDevitt High School in Glenside to work in a mail order house until he was drafted in January 1969. He did not do well in school but was a hard worker and stayed out of trouble. In the Army he was as a radio specialist and in his last letter, written on Nov. 14, he told his parents he was "counting the days to come home."

References:
http://www.virtualwall.org/dp/PastorinoMA01a.htm
http://www.thewall-usa.com/info.asp?recid=39639
http://www.vvmf.org/thewall/Wall_Id_No=39666

David Alan Patton
(Bristol)

United States Marine Corps
C Company, 1st Battalion, 26th Marine Regiment,
1st Marine Division

Rank: Private First Class (E-2), Enlisted
Length of Service: less than 1 year
MOS: 0311, Rifleman
Born: May 24, 1949
Died: Saturday, June 7, 1969
Age: 20
Circumstances: hostile; ground casualty; artillery, rocket or mortar
Location: Quang Nam Province (I Corps Tactical Zone)
Tour Started: January 6, 1969
Length of time in Vietnam: 152 days
Parents: survived by his mother and stepfather
Siblings: 2 sisters and 2 half-brothers
Marital Status: single
Religion: Protestant

High School: George Washington High School, Philadelphia PA (class of 1968)
Final resting place: Beverly National Cemetery
Location on The Wall: panel 23W, row 105

David is remembered by his family as "a happy-go-lucky kid who said he'd think about his future when he got out of the Marines." His family moved to Bucks County from Philadelphia about a month before their son died. On the day he died, President Nixon announced that 250,000 U.S. troops would be withdrawn in a plan to turn the war over to the South Vietnamese. He was a 1968 graduate of George Washington High School, where he earned letters in football and track.

References:
http://www.virtualwall.org/dp/PattonDA01a.htm
http://www.thewall-usa.com/info.asp?recid=39752
http://www.vvmf.org/thewall/Wall_Id_No=39779

Michael Charles Wunsch
(Feasterville)

United States Marine Corps
A Company, 3rd Tank Battalion, 3rd Marine Division

Recipient of the Silver Star

Rank: Captain (O-3), Enlisted
Length of Service: 3 years
MOS: 1802 Tank Officer
Born: March 16, 1944
Died: Monday, July 28, 1969 (during Operation Idaho Canyon and 10 days before he was due to return home)
Age: 25
Circumstances: hostile; ground casualty; other explosive device
Location: Quang Tri Province (I Corps Tactical Zone)

Tour Started: July 27, 1968
Length of time in Vietnam: 366 days
Marital Status: married to Diane
Religion: Protestant
College: United States Naval Academy
Location on The Wall: panel 20W, row 68

The synopsis of the Silver Star commendation:

The President of the United States takes pleasure in presenting the Silver Star Medal to Michael C. Wunsch (201349278), Captain, U.S. Marine Corps, for conspicuous gallantry and intrepidity in action while serving with Company A, 3d Tank Battalion, 3d Marine Division (Rein.), FMF, in connection with combat operations against the enemy in the Republic of Vietnam on July 27, 1969. By his courage, aggressive fighting spirit and steadfast devotion to duty in the face of extreme personal danger, Captain Wunsch upheld the highest traditions of the Marine Corps and the United States Naval Service.

A few of the remembrances posted for Michael:

Mike, you have been with me since that dreadful morning I was called to go identify your body. For many years I carried you with a guilt-ridden heart for not keeping you with me at Quang-Tri when you came by to say goodbye just hours before your untimely death. The sharing of C-Rats with you and having our last talk and laugh, and knowing how there was no way to convince you to stay with me, you were determined to go spend your last few hours with your beloved Marines in Con-Thien. It took seventeen long years to finally go face the Wall, and I thank God that I finally did touch you once again and release you to our Maker. You will always be

185

with me, my brother. You touched many Marines' hearts and left a part of you in all of us.

Capt. Wunsch was my C.O. of Alpha Co., 3rd tanks. I was a young corporal when he and the other brave men left us. I miss you Mike, and have thought about you over the years, too many times to count. I remember the personal talks we shared about home, while we served at Cam Lo, and Con Thien. You were a good man, and you made people feel at ease around you, when we had something important to talk about.

I graduated from the Naval Academy and underwent basic Marine training with Mike in 1967, then we went our separate ways in the Corps. He was one of the finest men and officers I have ever had the pleasure of knowing.

Michael was the Commander of the 15th Interrogator/Translator Team for six months or more before he was transferred to Tanks. He was such a gentleman, always looking out for his marines. I remember how much he wanted to get a Tank command. He had learned Mandarin Chinese at the Defense Language School.

After his tour in Vietnam, his next duty station was to be the US Naval Academy where was scheduled to teach Chinese to first year students.

Editor's note: Operation Idaho Canyon took place from July 21st to September 25th, 1969 in the Tam Ky area of Quang Tin Province. It involved elements of the 1st Marine Division and 101st Airborne Division.

References:
http://www.virtualwall.org/dw/WunschMC01a.htm
http://www.thewall-usa.com/info.asp?recid=57641
http://www.vvmf.org/thewall/Wall_Id_No=57592

1970

John Rodman Bloschichak
(Levittown)

United States Marine Corps
3rd Platoon, I Company, 3rd Battalion, 1st Marine Regiment,
1st Marine Division

Rank: Lance Corporal (E-3), Enlisted
Length of Service: 1 year
MOS: 0311, Rifleman
Born: August 23, 1951
Died: Friday, June 19, 1970
Age: 18
Circumstances: non-hostile; ground casualty; misadventure
(accidental homicide - friendly fire)
Location: Quang Nam Province (I Corps Tactical Zone)
Tour Started: February 15, 1970
Length of time in Vietnam: 124 days
Marital Status: single
Religion: Roman Catholic
Location on The Wall: panel 9W, row 67

References:
http://www.VirtualWall.org/db/BloschichakJR01a.htm
http://www.thewall-usa.com/info.asp?recid=4416
http://www.vvmf.org/thewall/Wall_Id_No=4440

William Douglas Booth
(Richboro)

United States Army
Headquarters & Headquarters Company,
USARV Engineering Command

Rank: Captain (O-3), Enlisted
Length of Service:
MOS: 2030, Aide-de-Camp
Engineering Command
Born: November 13, 1941
Died: Tuesday, May 12, 1970
Age: 28
Circumstances: hostile; air loss or crash over land; helicopter non-crew
Location: Pleiku Province (II Corps Tactical Zone)
Tour Started: January 4, 1970
Length of time in Vietnam: 128 days

Parents: William and Florence (Day)
Marital Status: single
Religion: Episcopal
High School: Council Rock High School, class of 1962
College: United States Military Academy, class of 1966
Final resting place: United States Military Academy
Location on The Wall: panel 10W, row 22

William was on his second tour in Vietnam and is remembered by his fellow soldiers as always fair, always the leader, and always a brave man who took care of his own. He was admired for his professionalism, dedication to duty, and hard work.

References:
http://www.VirtualWall.org/db/BoothWD01a.htm
http://www.thewall-usa.com/info.asp?recid=4751
http://www.vvmf.org/thewall/Wall_Id_No=4775

James Francis Brennan Jr.
(Levittown)

United States Navy
USS Ranger, VA-56, TF-77, CVW-2, 7th Fleet

Rank: Petty Officer 3rd Class (E-4), Enlisted
Length of Service: 1 year
MOS: Aviation Ordnanceman
Born: November 22, 1949
Died: Monday, January 5, 1970
Age: 20
Circumstances: non-hostile; ground casualty; died of illness or injury
Location: Quang Nam Province (I Corps Tactical Zone)

Tour Started: October 14, 1969
Length of time in Vietnam: 83 days (at sea)
Marital Status: single
Religion: Roman Catholic
High School: Bishop Egan High School, class of 1967
Final resting place: Beverly National Cemetery
Location on The Wall: panel 15W, row 128

James died in a Da Nang hospital of a spinal injury suffered
when he fell against the air intake of a jet plane's engine on
the aircraft carrier Ranger, off the Vietnam coast. He was
placing ordnance items aboard the plane at the time. He
enlisted March 22, 1968, and left aboard the Ranger on
October 14, 1969. His father said he "loved the Navy," and
wrote cheerful letters.

References:
http://www.VirtualWall.org/db/BrennanJF01a.htm
http://www.thewall-usa.com/info.asp?recid=5507
http://www.vvmf.org/thewall/Wall_Id_No=5531

Steven Richard Caucci
(Fairless Hills)

United States Army
C Battery, 1st Battalion, 321st Artillery Regiment,
101st Airborne Division

Rank: Private First Class (E-3), Drafted
Length of Service:
MOS: 13A10, Field Artillery Basic
Unit: C Battery, 1st Battalion, 321st Artillery Regiment, 101st
Airborne Division
Born: September 15, 1949
Died: Wednesday, August 5, 1970
Age: 20
Circumstances: non-hostile, died of illness or injury; ground
casualty; burns
Location: Thua Thien Province (I Corps Tactical Zone)

Tour Started: June 26, 1970
Length of time in Vietnam: 40 days
Parents: Mr. and Mrs. Alfred
Marital Status: single
Religion: Roman Catholic
Location on The Wall: panel 8W, row 84

References:
http://www.VirtualWall.org/dc/CaucciSR01a.htm
http://www.thewall-usa.com/info.asp?recid=8465
http://www.vvmf.org/thewall/Wall_Id_No=8481

Victor Monroe DeWalt
(Revere)

United States Marine Corps
I Company, 3rd Battalion, 1st Marine Regiment,
1st Marine Division

Rank: Lance Corporal (E-3), Enlisted
Length of Service: 1 year
MOS: 0311, Rifleman
Born: September 11, 1949
Died: Tuesday, November 10, 1970
Age: 21
Circumstances: non-hostile, died of illness or injury; ground casualty; accidental homicide
Location: Quang Nam Province (I Corps Tactical Zone)
Tour Started: May 10, 1970
Length of time in Vietnam: 184 days
Parents: Forrest and Aldine (Kain)
Marital Status: single
Final resting place: Greenwood Cemetery, Allentown PA

Location on The Wall: panel 6W, row 49

References:
http://www.VirtualWall.org/dd/DewaltVM01a.htm
http://www.thewall-usa.com/info.asp?recid=13096
http://www.vvmf.org/thewall/Wall_Id_No=12634

Glenn Harry English Jr.
(Cornwells Heights)

United States Army
E Company, 3rd Battalion, 503rd Infantry Regiment,
173rd Airborne Brigade

Recipient of the Medal of Honor

Rank: Staff Sergeant (E-6),
Length of Service:

MOS: 11F4P, Infantry Operations and Intelligence Specialist (Airborne Qualified)

Born: April 23, 1940

Died: Sunday, September 7, 1970

Age: 30

Circumstances: hostile; ground casualty; gun or small arms fire

Location: Binh Dinh Province (II Corps Tactical Zone)

Tour Started: August 24, 1970

Length of time in Vietnam: 14 days

Parents: Glenn Sr. and Betty Weining

Siblings: 1 brother (Larry), 3 sisters (Anna Mae and Linda)

Marital Status: married, 2 daughters – Debra and DeDe

Religion: Roman Catholic

Final resting place: Fort Bragg Post Cemetery

Location on The Wall: panel 7W, row 44

Glenn is a recipient of the Medal of Honor. The citation reads:

S/Sgt. English was riding in the lead armored personnel carrier in a 4-vehicle column when an enemy mine exploded in front of his vehicle. As the vehicle swerved from the road, a concealed enemy force waiting in ambush opened fire with automatic weapons and anti-tank grenades, striking the vehicle several times and setting it on fire. S/Sgt. English escaped from the disabled vehicle and, without pausing to extinguish the flames on his clothing, rallied his stunned unit. He then led it in a vigorous assault, in the face of heavy enemy automatic weapons fire, on the entrenched enemy position. This prompt and courageous action routed the enemy and saved his unit from destruction. Following the assault, S/Sgt. English heard the cries of 3 men still trapped inside the vehicle. Paying no heed to warnings that the ammunition and fuel in the burning personnel carrier might explode at any moment, S/Sgt. English raced to the vehicle and climbed inside to rescue his wounded comrades. As he was lifting 1 of the men to safety, the vehicle exploded, mortally wounding him and the man he was attempting to save. By his extraordinary devotion to duty, indomitable courage, and utter disregard for his own safety, S/Sgt. English saved his unit from destruction and selflessly sacrificed his life in a brave attempt to save 3 comrades. S/Sgt. English's conspicuous gallantry and intrepidity in action at the cost of his life were an inspiration to his comrades and are in the highest traditions of the U.S. Army.

August 8, 1974

Vietnam Victim Awarded Medal of Honor

The Congressional Medal of Honor has been awarded posthumously to Staff Sgt. Glenn H. English Jr. by President Gerald R. Ford. Sgt. English was killed in Vietnam in 1970.

Accepting the medal (top photo) are members of Sgt. English's family: his sister, Anna Mae Fike of Easton, Md. (holding boxed medal) and (rear left to right) Sgt. Larry English of Guam, brother; Mrs. Linda Wing of Sacramento, Calif., sister; and Mrs. Betty Weining, of Cleveland, Ohio, mother.

Sgt. English as a boy was a resident of the Williamsburg Children's Home for three years and lived for a time in the home of Mr. and Mrs. Herman Burket at Curryville, where his brother and a sister were foster children.

Also on hand for the medal presentation was the hero's father, Glenn H. English Sr. of Miami, Fla. Not present were the two daughters of Sgt. English, Debra, 8, and DeDe, 6.

The Army sergeant won the award for gallantry in action Sept. 7, 1970, in the Phu My district of South Vietnam. A citation accompanying the award reads, in part:

"Sgt. English was riding in the lead armored personnel carrier in a four-vehicle column when an enemy mine exploded in front of his vehicle. As the vehicle swerved from the road, a concealed enemy force waiting in ambush opened fire with automatic weapons and anti-tank grenades, striking the vehicle several times and setting it on fire.

"Sgt. English escaped from the disabled vehicle and, without pausing to extinguish the flames on his clothing, rallied his stunned unit. He then led it in a vigorous assault, in the face of heavy enemy automatic weapons fire, on the entrenched enemy position. This prompt and courageous action routed the enemy and saved his unit from destruction.

"Following the assault, Sgt. English heard the cries of three men still trapped inside the vehicle. Paying no heed to warnings that the ammunition and fuel in the burning personnel carrier might explode at any moment, Sgt. English raced to the vehicle, and climbed inside to rescue his wounded comrades. As he was lifting one o the men to safety, the vehicle exploded, mortally wounding him and the men he was attempting to save.

References:
http://www.history.army.mil/html/moh/vietnam-a-l.html
http://www.VirtualWall.org/de/EnglishGH01a.htm
http://www.thewall-usa.com/info.asp?recid=15130
http://www.vvmf.org/thewall/Wall_Id_No=15131

William James Erkes Jr.
(Pipersville)

United States Army
D Company, 3rd Battalion, 21st Infantry Regiment,
196th Infantry Brigade, Americal Division

Rank: 2nd Lieutenant (O-1),
Length of Service: less than 1 year
MOS: 1542, Infantry Unit Commander
Born: November 24, 1949
Died: Tuesday, January 7, 1970
Age: 20
Circumstances: hostile; ground casualty; gun or small arms fire
Location: Quang Tri Province (I Corps Tactical Zone)

Tour Started: December 6, 1969
Length of time in Vietnam: 32 days
Parents: William and Margaret (Day)
Siblings: 2 brothers
Marital Status: single
Religion: Baptist
High School: Palisades High School
College: Rutgers University
Location on The Wall: panel 14W, row 7

He was known as Jim to his friends and family. He was a top student at Palisades High School, president of his class and the student council. He was also editor of the school newspaper, an Eagle Scout and a licensed pilot (he soloed at the age of 16). He was a winner of a 4 year ROTC scholarship at Rutgers University. After one semester at Rutgers, he became disenchanted with college life because of the anti-war atmosphere that pervaded there. He decided to enlist in the Army and did so in April 1968. Had his vision been 20/20, he would have joined the Air Force. His father and both of his brothers were pilots.

In the Army he became an officer in the Green Berets. While on a search and destroy mission near Chu Lai, barely one month after he arrived in country, he was shot through the heart.

Prior to the Army he was involved in the orchard owned by his parents. He was planning on attending Delaware Valley College after the Army and then helping his parents run the orchard.

References:
http://www.VirtualWall.org/de/ErkesWJ01a.htm
http://www.thewall-usa.com/info.asp?recid=15223
http://www.vvmf.org/thewall/Wall_Id_No=15224
The Sunday Intelligencer, Vol. 96, No. 126, May 27, 1984

Robert Post Hampton Jr.

(Levittown)

United States Army
C Company, 1ˢᵗ Battalion, 61ˢᵗ Infantry Regiment,
5ᵗʰ Infantry Division

Rank: Sergeant (E-5) posthumous promotion, Enlisted
Length of Service:
MOS: 11B20, Infantryman
Born: September 7, 1951
Died: Monday, June 29, 1970
Age: 18
Circumstances: hostile; ground casualty; gun or small arms
fire
Location: Quang Tri Province (I Corps Tactical Zone)
Tour Started: November 13, 1969
Length of time in Vietnam: 228 days
Parents: Mr. & Mrs. Robert
Siblings: 2 brothers (Mike and John); 1 sister (Ginny)
Marital Status: single
Religion: Baptist
Final resting place: Beverly National Cemetery
Location on The Wall: panel 9W, row 101

References:
http://www.VirtualWall.org/dh/HamptonRP01a.htm
http://www.thewall-usa.com/info.asp?recid=21104
http://www.vvmf.org/thewall/Wall_Id_No=21090

Robert Oren Hill
(Churchville)

United States Army
237th Medical Detachment, 67th Medical Group,
44th Medical Brigade

Rank: Chief Warrant Officer (W-2), Enlisted
MOS: 100B, Utility/Observation Helicopter Pilot
Born: February 10, 1948
Died: Sunday, September 27, 1970
Age: 22
Circumstances: non-hostile; air loss; crash over land
Location: Quang Tri Province (I Corps Tactical Zone)
Tour Started: December 11, 1969
Length of time in Vietnam: 290 days
Parents: Robert and Elizabeth (Clapp)
Siblings: 1 brother (Bruce), 2 sisters (Cindy and Miriam)
Marital Status: single

Religion: Protestant
High School: Council Rock High School, class of 1965
Final resting place: North and Southampton Churchyard, Churchville PA
Location on The Wall: panel 7W row 95

Robert was a recipient of the Distinguished Flying Cross, Bronze Star, and Air Medal.

A tribute to Robert written by his brother Bruce:

Where do I start? He always wanted to fly and he was proud of the job he was doing - flying medical evacuation in the Phu Bai/Quang Tri area of I Corps. Bobby, born in Philadelphia, Pennsylvania on February 10th, 1948, was the oldest of two sons and two daughters. He grew up in Oreland and Churchville, Pennsylvania. He was a 1965 graduate from Council Rock High School in Newtown, Pennsylvania. After working for the Bell Telephone Company, he enlisted in the Army. Following graduation from helicopter flight school, he was sent to Germany for a year and then to Vietnam, where he served with the 237th and 571st Medical Detachments (DUSTOFF). For his service in Vietnam, he was awarded the Distinguished Flying Cross, Air Medal with sixteen oak leaf clusters, and the Bronze Star. Though only thirteen months apart, he is, was, and always will be, my "big brother." We served in Vietnam at the same time and were fortunate to get together several times. Those meetings are my most treasured memories. Each time we parted, he'd tell me "Be careful and keep your head down." He died two months after I got home. Even after 28 years, his death continues to haunt me and my two sisters. Laura Palmer, in the introduction to her book, Shrapnel in the Heart, states "Time occasionally makes loss more bearable. But for siblings, their own passage through life is a jarring reminder of just how much their brother missed."

This, perhaps, says it all for me. Many of our brothers never had the pleasure of going to college, marrying, buying a house, raising children, becoming grandparents. I truly miss what could have been: large family reunions, joint family vacations, picnics, holiday dinners together and all the other things that brothers do. We siblings are the survivors, but it's a long and often lonely road we travel. In many respects, time literally stopped with the notification of Bobby's death. Amid the pain and sadness, I will always have our wonderful childhood memories: the endless hours of ping pong and tennis, fun times camping and fishing, walks to the bus stop together, new bikes for Christmas, our favorite oldies from the early 60's, dating the Griffith sisters, and him teaching me to drive his '61 Chevy. If I could have him back, it would always be his turn to run the train set, and my turn to mow the lawn.

References:
http://www.virtualwall.org/dh/HillRO01a.htm
http://www.thewall-usa.com/info.asp?recid=23251
http://www.vvmf.org/thewall/Wall_Id_No=23231

David Charles Lownes
(Newtown)

United States Army
Headquarters & Headquarters Company, 3rd Battalion,
21st Infantry Regiment, 196th Infantry Brigade,
Americal Division

Rank: Private First Class (E-3), Drafted
Length of Service: less than 1 year
MOS: 91B10, Medical NCO
Born: December 27, 1949

Died: Friday, May 1, 1970
Age: 20
Circumstances: hostile; ground casualty
Location: Quang Tin Province (I Corps Tactical Zone)
Tour Started: January 6, 1970
Length of time in Vietnam: 115 days
Parents: Mr. & Mrs. Charles
Marital Status: single
Religion: Presbyterian
Location on The Wall: panel 11W, row 81

A former comrade of Charles wrote:

*"Charles, you are remembered for the sacrifice you made in
Hiep Duc Valley forty years ago. As a medic you assisted the
wounded without regard to your personal safety. A grateful
nation and the guys of Company A 3/21 Infantry have not
forgotten you and the others who fell that night."*

References:
http://www.VirtualWall.org/dl/LownesCD01a.htm
http://www.thewall-usa.com/info.asp?recid=31365
http://www.vvmf.org/thewall/Wall_Id_No=31423

Nelson Charles Luther
(Warminster)

United States Army
Service Battery, 6th Battalion, 32nd Artillery, 23rd Artillery Group,
I Field Force

Rank: Staff Sergeant (E-6), Enlisted
Length of Service:
MOS: 76Y40, Unit Supply Sergeant
Born: August 29, 1941
Died: Saturday, May 9, 1970
Age: 28
Circumstances: non-hostile; ground casualty; vehicle loss or crash
Location: Phu Yen Province (II Corps Tactical Zone)
Tour Started: October 28, 1968
Length of time in Vietnam: 558 days

Parents: Marshall and Mary Luther
Marital Status: married
Religion: Methodist
High School: Council Rock High School
Final resting place: Union Cemetery, Richboro PA
Location on The Wall: panel 10W, row 7

References:
http://www.VirtualWall.org/dl/LutherNC01a.htm
http://www.thewall-usa.com/info.asp?recid=31594
http://www.vvmf.org/thewall/Wall_Id_No=31650

Paul F.C. Marsh
(Bristol)

The editors were unable to find any information on Paul Marsh.

Frank Martin Mebs
(Newtown)

United States Army
A Company, 27th Engineering Battalion, 45th Engineering Group, 18th Engineering Brigade, USARV Engineering Command

Rank: Specialist 5th Class (E-5), Enlisted
Length of Service:
MOS: 62E20, Heavy Construction Equipment Operator
Born: September 13, 1949

Died: Wednesday, May 27, 1970
Age: 20
Circumstances: hostile; ground casualty; misadventure (friendly fire)
Location: Thua Thien Province (I Corps Tactical Zone)
Tour Started: November 20, 1968
Length of time in Vietnam: 553 days
Parents: Martin and Dorothy (Arnwine)
Marital Status: single
Religion: Roman Catholic
High School: Council Rock High School
Location on The Wall: panel 10W, row 110

A former comrade of Franks' wrote this about him:

He saved a lot of lives, maybe mine. I was with C battery 1/83 artillery unit, an 8" and 175 MM self-propelled guns. We were on the north end of FSB Veghel. We had just moved up and had no bunkers. On the night of May 27 I was awakened by a flash followed by a massive explosion. The next morning we learned that an ammo dump had caught fire. The ammo dump was about in the middle of Vegel, right in front of a 155 battery. Two dozers and 20 some soldiers tried to put the fire out. The fire got out of hand everyone took cover except Frank Mebs. He stayed on his dozer and smothered the explosion. Nothing was left of the dozer except the blade and some parts. We did some calculations. If Frank hadn't smothered the explosion the 155 battery may have gone up followed by a 105 battery immediately north of the dump and then our battery. Because of Frank's heroism only one other person was killed.

References:
http://www.VirtualWall.org/dm/MebsFM01a.htm
http://www.thewall-usa.com/info.asp?recid=34591
http://www.vvmf.org/thewall/Wall_Id_No=33303

David John Ortals
(Levittown)

United States Marine Corps
Headquarters & Maintenance Squadron, Marine Aircraft Group 11, 1st Marine Aircraft Wing

Rank: Corporal (E-4), Enlisted
Length of Service: 3 years
MOS: 6014, Unmanned Aerial Vehicle Mechanic
Born: February 6, 1948
Died: Friday, May 22, 1970
Age: 22
Circumstances: non-hostile; ground casualty; died of other causes – drowned or suffocated
Location: Quang Nam Province (I Corps Tactical Zone)
Tour Started: December 6, 1969
Length of time in Vietnam: 167 days

Parents: Roman & Winifred
Marital Status: married
Religion: Roman Catholic
Location on The Wall: panel 10W, row 83

References:
http://www.VirtualWall.org/do/OrtalsDJ01a.htm
http://www.thewall-usa.com/info.asp?recid=38790
http://www.vvmf.org/thewall/Wall_Id_No=38832

Glenn Dale Rickert
(Sellersville)

United States Army
Headquarters Company, 11th Infantry Brigade,
Americal Division

Recipient of the Distinguished Flying Cross (2 awards), Bronze Star, Air Medal, and Army Commendation Medal.

Rank: Captain (O-3),
Length of Service: 3 years
MOS: 1981, Rotary Wing Aviation Unit Commander
Born: August 23, 1945
Died: Friday, May 29, 1970
Age: 24
Circumstances: hostile; air loss or crash over land
Location: Quang Ngai Province (I Corps Tactical Zone)

Tour Started: November 20, 1969
Length of time in Vietnam: 190 days
Parents: Valentine & Mary
Siblings:
Marital Status: married to Margie (Kulp), 1 son (Glenn Jr.)

Religion: Protestant
High School: Souderton High School, class of 1963

College: Temple University, class of 1966, Chemical Engineering
Location on The Wall: panel 10W, row 118

He is remembered by former flight school classmates as a nice guy, always going out of his way to help someone.

On the morning of May 29, 1970, Glenn climbed behind the controls of a light observation helicopter and lifted off to take part in a combat assault operation. The attach was to take place close to the village of Tan Phu, located about 13 miles southwest of Quang Ngai City in Quang Ngai Province. At the target area, Glenn's ship came under intense small arms fire and crashed when he was hit twice, mortally wounded.

Glenn was the youngest of three children and his mother recalled that he was never in any trouble. Sports were Glenn's primary interests as a youth. He was on the wrestling team at Souderton high school and played second base in American Legion baseball. He tried to play football but was deemed to be too small for that sport. Glenn had also been a baseball coach with the Souderton Community Little League.

He was a serious student at Temple University, always working at his lessons. Upon graduation and finding a tight job market, Glenn enlisted in the Army. His high scores on placement tests earned him a place at Officers Candidate School. After graduation from that he decided he wanted to be a helicopter pilot.

When Glenn was first sent to Vietnam he was assigned to a desk job. It didn't take long for him to want to be in the thick of things and he requested flight duty.

In his last letter home to his wife, Glenn ended it with, *"I'm going to sign off, knowing that our Lord and Savior is keeping you and Glenn under his wings: I know he is helping me considerably and his presence is felt at all times. All my love forever, Glenn."*

References:
http://www.virtualwall.org/dr/RickertGD01a.htm
http://www.thewall-usa.com/info.asp?recid=43340
http://www.vvmf.org/thewall/Wall_Id_No=43355
The Sunday Intelligencer, Vol. 96, No. 126, May 27, 1984

Boyd Leroy Shook
(Yardley)

United States Army
Unit: 59th Engineering Company, 39th Engineering Battalion,
45th Engineering Group, 18th Engineering Brigade,
USARV Engineering Command

Rank: Corporal (E-4) posthumous promotion, Enlisted
Length of Service:
MOS: 62B20, Construction Equipment Repairer
Born: April 10, 1952
Died: Tuesday, July 28, 1970
Age: 18
Circumstances: non-hostile; died of other causes; vehicle loss
or crash

Location: Quang Ngai Province (I Corps Tactical Zone)
Tour Started: May 9, 1970
Length of time in Vietnam: 80 days
Siblings: 1 brother (Al); 1 sister (Lori)
Marital Status: single
Location on The Wall: panel 8W, row 63

References:
http://www.VirtualWall.org/ds/ShookBL01a.htm
http://www.thewall-usa.com/info.asp?recid=47261
http://www.vvmf.org/thewall/Wall_Id_No=47260

Robert James Weidle

(Cornwells Heights)

United States Army
D Company, 3rd Battalion, 1st Infantry Regiment,
11th Infantry Brigade, Americal Division

Rank: Private First Class (E-3),
Length of Service:
MOS: 11D10, Armor Reconnaissance Specialist
Born: September 6, 1950
Died: Wednesday, September 2, 1970
Age: 19
Circumstances: hostile; ground casualty; artillery, rocket or mortar
Location: Quang Ngai Province (I Corps Tactical Zone)

Tour Started: July 20, 1970
Length of time in Vietnam: 44 days
Marital Status: single
Religion: Roman Catholic
Location on The Wall: panel 7W, row 35

References:
http://www.VirtualWall.org/dw/WeidleRJ01a.htm
http://www.thewall-usa.com/info.asp?recid=55094
http://www.vvmf.org/thewall/Wall_Id_No=55054

Thomas Williams
(Bristol)

The editors could not find any information on Thomas
Williams.

Richard C. Williams
(Levittown)

United States Army
D Company, 2nd Battalion, 14th Infantry Regiment,
25th Infantry Division

Rank: Private First Class (E-3), Drafted
Length of Service: less than 1 year
MOS: 11B10, Infantryman
Born: January 18, 1946
Died: Sunday, January 4, 1970
Age: 23
Circumstances: hostile; ground casualty; other explosive device
Location: Binh Duong Province (III Corps Tactical Zone)
Tour Started: December 2, 1969
Length of time in Vietnam: 23 days
Parents: James and Elizabeth
Siblings: none
Marital Status: single
Religion: Protestant
High School: Pennsbury High School, class of 1963

College: Cornell University
Location on The Wall: panel 15W, row 127

Richard was killed by a booby trap Sunday, January 4 while on a combat mission only five weeks after being sent to Vietnam. In a letter received Saturday, January 3 by his parents, James F. and Elizabeth Williams, he mentioned the slaying of an enemy soldier by his unit, saying photos of the soldier's wife and children were found on the body. "I'm against killing anyone," Richard wrote. "This man was a human being, too." He was a graduate of Cornell University with a master's degree in business administration. Prior to his induction, Richard was an auditor for Sylvania Corp. in Syracuse. He also was a Pennsbury High School graduate.

References:
http://www.virtualwall.org/dw/WilliamsRC04a.htm
http://www.thewall-usa.com/info.asp?recid=56459
http://www.vvmf.org/thewall/Wall_Id_No=56414

1971

Mark Afflerbach

(Levittown)

United States Army
F Troop, 8th Cavalry Regiment, Americal Division

Recipient of the Air Medal

Rank: Captain (O-3), Reserve
MOS: 61204, Armored Reconnaissance Unit Commander (Pilot)
Born: July 8, 1945
Died: Sunday, March 7, 1971
Age: 25
Circumstances: non-hostile; died of other causes; air loss or crash over land
Location: Quang Tri Province (I Corps Tactical Zone)
Tour Started: November 27, 1970
Length of time in Vietnam: 100 days
Marital Status: married
Religion: Roman Catholic
High School:
College:
Final resting place: Arlington National Cemetery
Location on The Wall: panel 4W, row 30

Accident Summary: *AT 1730 HOURS, 7 MARCH 1971, AIRCRAFT 69-16438 AN AH-1G DEPARTED THE F TROOP, 8TH CAVALRY AREA IN QUANG TRI FOR A VISUAL RECONNAISSANCE MISSION SUPPORT OF C COMPANY 2ND BATTALION 502D INFANTRY 101ST AIRBORNE DIVION. AFTER APPROXIMATELY ONE(1) HOUR OF NORMAL VISUAL RECONNAISSANCE, AIRCRAFT 69-16438 EXPERIENCED A MAIN ROTOR HUB ASSEMBLY SEPARATION AT AN ALTIDUDE OF 700 FEET MSL. THE*

AIRCRAFT STRUCK THE GROUN AT AN ANGLE OF APPROXIMATELY 90 DEGREES TO THE SLOPE OF THE TERRAIN, HEADING APPROXIMATELY 270 DEGREES. IT THEN EXPERIENCED POST CRASH FIRE AND EXPLOSION FROM UNEXPENDED FUEL AND ORDANCE.

An old neighborhood friend recalls Mark:

"I well remember him as a good-natured pleasant fellow but one who would stand his ground. All these years past, still I painfully and vividly remember finding him sitting on the curb nursing a very bloodied nose. He had been minding his own business in his own front yard when two males from another neighborhood showed up to engage some of their bully tactics. It would have been so easy, and 'sensible', for Mark to retreat to the house. Mark chose otherwise and took a beating for his principles. I also witnessed him 'taking-up' for others being harassed."

References:
http://www.virtualwall.org/da/AfflerbachMx01a.htm
http://www.thewall-usa.com/info.asp?recid=316
http://www.vvmf.org/thewall/Wall_Id_No=358

Patrick John Breslin
(Sellersville)

United States Army
176th Assault Helicopter Company,
Americal Division

Recipient of the Air Medal

Rank: Specialist 4th Class (E-4), Enlisted
MOS: 67A1F, Aircraft Maintenance Apprentice (Flight)
Born: September 11, 1952
Died: Monday, October 18, 1971
Age: 19
Circumstances: non-hostile; died of other causes; air loss, crash at sea
Location: Quang Tin Province (I Corps Tactical Zone)
Tour Started: May 14, 1971
Length of time in Vietnam: 157 days
Siblings: 1 sister
Marital Status: single
Religion: Roman Catholic
High School: Pennridge High School, class of 1970
Location on The Wall: panel 2W, row 42

Patrick graduated from Pennridge High School in Perkasie, in 1970, and entered the Army that fall. He was ordered to Viet Nam in May 1971 and assigned to the 176th Assault Helicopter Company of the 23rd Infantry (AMERICAL) Division. The specialist four, a helicopter crew chief and door gunner, died on October 18, 1971, when his aircraft was hit and crashed in the South China Sea. He was 19 years old. Breslin was survived by his parents and a sister.

On the evening of 17 October 1971, aircraft UH-1H tail number 68-15237 was assigned the night perimeter mission for the Chu Lai defense command. The crew consisted of

- 1LT Robert Jameson Barton, pilot;
- WO L N Pate, copilot;
- SP4 Patrick John Breslin, gunner;
- SP4 Wesley Stewart Shelton, crew chief; and
- a Vietnamese national, name unknown.

The mission entailed flying at 300 feet MSL or below, checking the perimeter with landing and search light. 1LT Barton wanted to remain on 5 minute standby because he felt the weather was too bad to fly, but launched at 2230 hours. After arriving on station the weather was found to be better than expected and the mission was continued. The aircraft landed and refueled before midnight, but after arriving back on station in deteriorating weather the division tactical operations center decided to allow the Huey to return to the airfield and go on 5 minute alert.

One more pattern around the perimeter was flown before landing. As the Huey circled around the northern side of the base, where an over-water leg was necessary, the crew heard a loud thump. According to the only survivor (WO Pate), 1LT Barton commented "Don't worry, we only hit a bird. I hit one last night."

WO Pate leaned to his right and lowered his head to look at the engine instruments to see if there were any abnormal instrument readings. While he had his head lowered the aircraft struck the water. WO Pate remembered the airspeed indicator reading 80 knots just prior to the accident. The crash was heard by a bunker guard on duty approximately 300 meters from the crash site, who reported the mishap to his superiors, who in turn reported it to division and a search and rescue was put into motion. Two medevac aircraft and a flare ship were dispatched but the weather had become extremely hazardous and the SAR effort failed to locate either the wreckage or the crew.

Warrant Officer Pate was recovered alive at dawn, some 4000 meters south of the crash site. The bodies of the other four men aboard the Huey were recovered.

References:
http://www.virtualwall.org/db/BreslinPJ01a.htm
http://www.thewall-usa.com/info.asp?recid=5536
http://www.vvmf.org/thewall/Wall_Id_No=5560

Robert Howard Maggs
(Lahaska)

Robert Howard Maggs

United States Army
A Company, 1st Battalion, 46th Infantry Regiment,
196th Infantry Brigade, Americal Division

Rank: Private First Class (E-3), Drafted
MOS: 11B10, Infantryman
Born: August 9, 1948
Died: Friday, October 1, 1971
Age: 23
Circumstances: non-hostile; ground casualty; other accident
Location: Quang Nam Province (I Corps Tactical Zone)
Tour Started: August 18, 1971
Length of time in Vietnam: 44 days
Marital Status: married to Patricia (Vorhauer)
Religion: Baptist
High School: Woodrow Wilson High School, class of 1966

Location on The Wall: panel 2W, row 32

A former member of his unit remembers Robert:

He went by the nick-name "Goofy Grape" had been in the bush for a few weeks then sent to FB Linda I think? The other FB we worked near was Maude. He was involved in an accident, something with fuel. A week or so after he left for the FB we heard he had been hurt, then a few days later we heard that he had died. He was an RTO (Radio Telephone Operator) in the bush, if I remember correctly? Was a good Grunt, he had a real zingy sense of humor. We had a memorial ceremony for him when we went in the rear 2-3 weeks later. We were working the area west of DaNang (Charlie Ridge, Happy Valley up to Elephant Valley and out some 15-20 miles), the range for the Rockets they were using at the time.

References:
http://www.virtualwall.org/dm/MaggsRH01a.htm
http://www.thewall-usa.com/info.asp?recid=31929
http://www.vvmf.org/thewall/Wall_Id_No=31943

James Paul Markey Jr.
(Warminster)

United States Army
43rd Infantry Platoon, Scout Dog,
5th Infantry Division

Recipient of the Bronze Star

Rank: Private First Class (E-3), Drafted
Length of Service:

MOS: 11B10, Infantryman
Born: June 4, 1947
Died: Tuesday, January 26, 1971
Age: 23
Circumstances: hostile; ground casualty; other explosive device
Location: Quang Tri Province (I Corps Tactical Zone)
Tour Started: November 23, 1970
Length of time in Vietnam: 64 days
Marital Status: married to Judith (Gather)
Religion: Protestant
High School: Neshaminy High School, class of 1965
Location on The Wall: panel 5W, row 65

James was a Mine Dog Handler and was awarded the Bronze Star for merit. He is remembered by former classmates as having a sunny smile and a happy go lucky disposition. He was a person who brightened your life.

References:
http://www.virtualwall.org/dm/MarkeyJP01a.htm
http://www.thewall-usa.com/info.asp?recid=32387
http://www.vvmf.org/thewall/Wall_Id_No=32397

Martin Terrance McDonald

(Langhorne)

United States Army
Headquarters & Headquarters Company, 2nd Battalion,
503rd Infantry Regiment, 173rd Airborne Brigade

Recipient of the Distinguished Service Cross

Rank: Sergeant (E-5), Enlisted
Length of Service:
MOS: 91B2P, Medical NCO (Airborne)
Born: December 15, 1950
Died: Saturday, April 10, 1971
Age: 20
Circumstances: hostile; ground casualty; gun or small arms fire
Location: Binh Dinh Province (II Corps Tactical Zone)
Tour Started: March 18, 1970
Length of time in Vietnam: 388 days
Parents: Martin and Ann (Munnell)
Siblings: 1 brother, 2 sisters

Marital Status: single
Religion: Roman Catholic
College: University of Pennsylvania
Location on The Wall: panel 4W, row 116

Doc McDonald was a Medic. It was in his heart, his head, and his hands. He was killed in action while performing life-saving first aid on a member of his Recon Team, earning the Distinguished Service Cross posthumously.

Citation: The President of the United States takes pride in presenting the Distinguished Service Cross (Posthumously) to Martin Terrance McDonald (190-40-5995), Specialist Fourth Class, U.S. Army, for extraordinary heroism in connection with military operations involving conflict with an armed hostile force in the Republic of Vietnam, while serving with Headquarters and Headquarters Company, 2d Battalion, 503d Infantry, 173d Airborne Brigade. Specialist Four McDonald distinguished himself by exceptionally valorous actions on 10 April 1971. On that date Specialist McDonald was serving as a medical aidman for a six man reconnaissance team on an offensive mission in Phu My District, when the team was taken under fire by an estimated platoon-sized enemy force. The enemy-initiated contact included rockets, machinegun and automatic small arms fire. In the initial hail of fire, the team leader was severely wounded, and the remainder of the team was halted a short distance away, leaving him in an open, vulnerable position. Specialist McDonald, although wounded himself during the initial contact, realized the extreme danger his team leader was in and, with total disregard for his personal safety, exposed himself to the intense enemy fire and ran to the aid of his fallen team leader. He then placed himself between the team leader and the enemy and began returning fire. An incoming rocket landed nearby, wounding him for the second time as the force of the explosion knocked him to the ground. He immediately recovered and rolled over on his team leader to protect him from the enemy fire. Realizing that further movement was impossible, Specialist McDonald stood up between the enemy and the severely wounded man and began placing accurate semi-automatic fire upon the enemy positions, until he was mortally wounded by an enemy rocket. Specialist Four McDonald's extraordinary heroism and devotion to duty, at the cost of his life, were in keeping with the highest traditions of the military service and reflect great credit upon himself, his unit, and the United States Army. Department of the Army, General Orders No. 32 (August 3, 1972)

"Terry" McDonald had attended the University Of Pennsylvania for a semester before he joined the Army in December 1968. He planned to return to Penn when he completed his military obligation. He had been a volunteer fireman in suburban Bucks County.

References:
http://www.virtualwall.org/dm/McdonaldMT01a.htm
http://www.thewall-usa.com/info.asp?recid=33722
http://www.vvmf.org/thewall/Wall_Id_No=36529

Charles Paul Montross

(Warminster)

United States Army
C Company, 75th Support Battalion, 5th Infantry Division

Rank: Sergeant (E-5) posthumous promotion, Drafted
MOS: 45K20, Armament Repairer
Born: February 6, 1950
Died: Thursday, February 11, 1971
Age: 21
Circumstances: hostile; ground casualty; misadventure (friendly fire)
Location: Quang Tri Province (I Corps Tactical Zone)
Tour Started: April 16, 1970
Length of time in Vietnam: 291 days
Parents: Robert & Reba
Siblings: 2 brothers, 3 sisters

Marital Status: married to Linda (Shum)
Religion: Roman Catholic
High School: William Tennant High School
Final resting place: Beulah Cemetery, New Britain PA
Location on The Wall: panel 5W, row 96

He quit high school in the 11th grade to work at a machine shop. He liked the music of Elvis Presley and he liked cars. Charles did not want to join the Army. When he was drafted, his wife urged him to go to Canada to escape. Three members of his family had been in the Army and that tradition made him stay and serve. He was married for just one week when he left for Vietnam. He died when an enemy rocket struck his bunker at Vandegrift Combat Base.

References:
http://www.virtualwall.org/dm/MontrossCP01a.htm
http://www.thewall-usa.com/info.asp?recid=36036
http://www.vvmf.org/thewall/Wall_Id_No=34743
The Sunday Intelligencer, Vol. 96, No. 126, May 27, 1984

William Charles Vasey

(Doylestown)

United States Navy
73rd RVN RAID, Naval Advisory Group

Rank: Lieutenant (O-3), Enlisted
Length of Service: 4 years
MOS: 1100, Unrestricted Line Officer (Surface Warfare)
Born: November 2, 1944
Died: Thursday, January 7, 1971
Age: 26
Circumstances: hostile; ground casualty; other explosive device
Location: Kien Giang Province (IV Corps Tactical Zone)
Marital Status: single
Religion: Protestant
Location on The Wall: panel 5W, row 32

References:
http://www.virtualwall.org/dv/VaseyWC01a.htm

http://www.thewall-usa.com/info.asp?recid=53490
http://www.vvmf.org/thewall/Wall_Id_No=53461

1972

Ronald Anthony Longfellow
(Chalfont)

United States Army
Aero Rifle Platoon, Air Cavalry Troop,
11th Armored Cavalry Regiment

Rank: Specialist 4th Class (E-4), Drafted
Length of Service:
MOS: 11B10, Infantryman
Born: September 22, 1951
Died: Wednesday, January 19, 1972
Age: 20
Circumstances: hostile; ground casualty; other explosive device
Location: Bien Hoa Province (III Corps Tactical Zone)
Tour Started: September 6, 1971

Length of time in Vietnam: 135 days
Parents: Charles and Ruth
Siblings: 4 brothers (Charles, Duane, Kenneth, and Jerry), 5 sisters (Marilyn, Carol, Jane, Linda, and Janice)
Marital Status: single
Religion: Roman Catholic
High School: Central Bucks High School, class of 1970
Final resting place: Whitemarsh Memorial Park
Location on The Wall: panel 2W, row 99

RONALD A LONGFELLOW ·

"Ronny wasn't afraid of anything. He really didn't know the meaning of fear," Duane Longfellow of Chalfont said of his brother Ronald, the last man from Bucks County listed killed in the Vietnam War.

Ronald Longfellow accepted his draft notice philosophically, said his mother, Ruth. He said he was anxious to do his two years of service in the Army, go to Vietnam and return home to get on with his life.

Ronald worked with this father at Trailmobile Division of Pullman Inc. in West Point, Montgomery County, after graduating from Central Bucks West High School in 1970. He also "practically lived" at Pit-Catcher Lanes in Chalfont, which he managed. Ronald loved to bowl, play pool, ride his motorcycle and keep the kids from the neighborhood out of trouble, his mother said.

"He wanted to get the war over with, come home, get back to his job, marry his girlfriend and live happily ever after," his mother said.

Army Pfc. Ronald Longfellow, 20, son of Mr. and Mrs. Charles Phillip Longfellow, 26 Valley View Drive, Chalfont, died Wednesday in the 24th Evacuation Hospital, Long Bihn, South Vietnam.

Longfellow, a 1967 Central Bucks High School graduate, had been in the hospital since Dec. 28, when he stepped on a land mine while acting as point man on an infantry patrol just north of Bein Hoa, near Saigon.

Drafted in April, when he was working in the service parts department of Trailmobile Division of Pullman, Inc., West Point, Longfellow had served first with the 101st Airborne Division, then was selected for duty with an Air Cavalry Rifle Patrol Squadron, the unit in which he was serving when wounded.

Two brothers are serving in the U.S. Navy, Charles Longfellow Jr., Guantanamo, Cuba, and Duane Longfellow, hospitalized with an illness he contracted in Vietnam at the Naval hospital, Bethesda, Md.

RONALD A. LONGFELLOW

At home are brothers Kenneth and Jerry; and sisters, Marilyn, Carol, Jane, Linda and Janice.

References:

http://www.virtualwall.org/dl/LongfellowRA01a.htm
http://www.thewall-usa.com/info.asp?recid=31111
http://www.vvmf.org/thewall/Wall_Id_No=31169
The Sunday Intelligencer, Vol. 96, No. 126, May 27, 1984

One who should be on the wall

William Stanley Geary

(Roslyn)

WILLIAM STANLEY GEARY
"Bill"

Wrightstown   6/22/45
Noted yodler . . . political devotee . . .
organized student council elections . . .
friendly . . . adroit 4-H worker.
Chorus 10, 11, 12; Baseball 11; Bucks
County Chorus 11, 12; District Chorus 12.

United States Marine Corps
3rd Platoon, I Company, 3rd Battalion, 1st Marine Regiment,
1st Marine Division

Rank: 2nd Lieutenant (O-1), Reserve
Length of Service: less than 1 year
MOS: 0301, Basic Infantry Officer
Born: June 22, 1945
Died: Saturday, April 5, 1969
Age: 23
Circumstances: hostile; ground casualty; gun or small arms fire
Location: Quang Nam Province (I Corps Tactical Zone)

Tour Started: February 16, 1969
Length of time in Vietnam: 48 days
Siblings: 1 brother (John)
Marital Status: single
Religion: Roman Catholic
High School: Council Rock High School
Final resting place: Holy Sepulchre Cemetery, Philadelphia PA
Location on The Wall: panel 27W, row 17

On 05 April 1969 India, Kilo, and Lima Companies, 3/1 Marines, were conducting sweeps in Quang Nam Province. At 1120, Lima began a river crossing and found themselves taking fire from a tree line on the opposite side of the river. India 3/1 was in a position to take the enemy in the flank and proceeded to do so - but by 1330 had found the enemy well entrenched and willing to fight. India 3/1 pressed the attack and by 1500 had forced the NVA to withdraw, leaving 72 bodies behind. The assault had been costly, though, with 9 men killed and 32 wounded in the action. William was one of those killed.

A childhood friend remembers William:

Butch was my friend when we were boys in the little south Jersey town of Clementon. We went swimming together in Silver Lake and we played baseball - badly as I remember. He had freckles and a smile so big it would light up any room. Of one thing I am certain, as a boy, as a person, he was better than I was. And now he always will be. Both of our fathers were Marines.

In honor of William's work with the 4H Club, a memorial was dedicated to him, in August 2008, at the grounds of the Middletown Grange Fair.

References:
http://www.virtualwall.org/dg/GearyWS01a.htm
http://www.thewall-usa.com/info.asp?recid=18176
http://www.vvmf.org/thewall/Wall_Id_No=18165

Missing In Action

Donald Richard Kemmerer
(Quakertown)

United States Air Force
390th Tactical Fighter Squadron, 366th Tactical Fighter Wing, 7th Air Force

Recipient of the Air Medal

Rank: Major (O-4) promoted while in MIA status, Reserve
Length of Service:
MOS: 1115A, Pilot
Born: May 20, 1941
Died: August 6, 1967 (incident date)
Age: 26
Circumstances: hostile; air loss or crash over land
Location: North Vietnam
Tour Started:
Length of time in Vietnam:
Parents: Donald Campbell Kemmerer and Mary (Blank)
Siblings: 1 sister (Donna)
Marital Status: married to Marsha Ann (Keiper); 1 son Michael Scott

Religion: Lutheran
High School: class of 1960
College: Penn State University
Location on The Wall: panel 24E, row 83

A high school classmate remembers Donald:

Dick was one of the good ones. Always there to lend a hand when we were growing up in Quakertown, PA. Always the 'level headed' teen in our group. The clean cut high schooler that always sent the girls swooning! We graduated in 1960, and at every reunion, Dick is fondly remembered.

Circumstances of his loss:

Capt. Donald R. Kemmerer and Capt. Albert L. Page, Jr. were co-pilots of an F4C fighter jet dispatched from Da Nang on a strike mission over North Vietnam on August 6, 1967. Their aircraft was the lead plane in a two-aircraft flight. When Page and Kemmerer were over the target, their aircraft was seen to be hit by hostile fire. Page and Kemmerer radioed that they were ejecting while the aircraft was still near the target area. One engine was observed to be on fire, and the aircraft crashed in the water. The flight was, at that time, about 10 miles north of the city of Vinh Linh in Quang Binh Province, North Vietnam. The aircraft crashed less than 5 miles offshore. No parachutes had been observed exiting the failing aircraft, nor had emergency radio beeper signals been heard. It was not certain if either crewman safely exited the aircraft, but as death was not confirmed, the two were classified Missing in Action.

References:
http://www.virtualwall.org/dk/KemmererDR01a.htm
http://www.thewall-usa.com/info.asp?recid=27630

Walter Harris Sigafoos III
(Richboro)

United States Air Force
421st Tactical Fighter Squadron

Recipient of the Air Medal

Rank: Captain (O-3), Enlisted
Length of Service: 3 years
MOS: 1551F, Weapons System Officer
Born: August 29, 1946
Died: October 9, 1973
Age:
Circumstances: hostile; air loss or crash over land
Location: Laos
Tour Started: April 25, 1971

248

Length of time in Vietnam:
Parents: Mr. & Mrs. Walter Harris Sigafoos Jr.
Siblings: 1 brother (Alan)
Marital Status: married to Judy; 1 son Walter Harris Sigafoos IV
Religion:
High School: Council Rock High School, class of 1964

College: United States Air Force Academy, class of 1968
Final resting place: military marker at United States Air Force Academy Cemetery, Colorado Springs, CO
Location on The Wall: panel 3W, row 12

WALTER HARRISON SIGAFOOS III   "Foos"

After spending eighteen leisurely years in the greenery of Pennsylvania, Walt journeyed to the brown hills of USAFA, deciding that the Air Force had more use for him than the U. of Delaware. He has managed to spread his talents around quite a bit here by serving stints in the Tough Twenty Trolls, Fightin' Fourth, and finally, Thirsty Third. He got interested in skiing and became Secretary and then President of the Ski Club. Majoring in astro, he managed to make Dean's List a couple of times. Foos served very ably as a member of the COC's Drill Team under the Western Skies of Colorado. Future plans include Blind Man's Pilot Training in California and graduate school. Walt's four years at USAFA only go to show that "you can take the kid out of Philly, but you can't take the Philly out of the kid."

W. H. Sigafoos III

Walter graduated from the Academy with a major in Astronautics. He was named to the Superintendent's Merit List in his second class year. He was elected president of the Ski Club and was a member of the Dance Committee. Following graduation he attended UNT at Mather AFB and graduated as a Distinguished Graduate. He received combat crew training in the F-4 at George AFB and was subsequently assigned with the 45th TFW at Mac-Dill AFB. In March 1971 he was reassigned to the 421st TFS at Da Nang Airfield, RVN. Walter was awarded the Distinguished Flying Cross, the Air Medal and the Purple Heart.

A remembrance from a fellow classmate at the Air Force Academy:

Walter was an upperclassman during my first summer at the academy. He demonstrated a great balance of exemplary mentorship, discipline, and compassion with new basics. I have fond memories of Walter from a work detail I served on under him that first summer of 1967 at USAFA. It was a privilege to wear his bracelet until his death declaration.

Circumstances of the loss:

On 25 April 1971, Capt. Jeffrey C. "Jeff" Lemon, pilot; and then 1st Lt. Walter H. Sigafoos, Weapons Systems Officer; comprised the crew of an F4D (serial #66-7616), call sign "Gunfighter 14," that departed DaNang Airbase as the lead aircraft in a flight of two. Their mission was a night escort/strike mission to interdict enemy traffic moving along the infamous Ho Chi Minh Trail. Weather conditions at the time of loss were clear with no moon and approximately 2 miles visibility.

Gunfighter flight proceeded to rendezvous with an AC119 gunship over their area of operation. After 30 minutes of escort duty, Gunfighter 14 departed the area to refuel from an airborne tanker. The flight returned to the target area approximately an hour later to relieve their wingman, Gunfighter 16 that was performing the same escort function for the gunship. Shortly thereafter the AC119 located an enemy truck traveling along Highway 165, a primary road running generally north/south through the rugged jungle covered mountains of eastern Laos located approximately 5 miles west of Tang Pong. Approximately 18 miles south of the target location, Highway 165 turns to the east and enters South Vietnam south of Kham Duc.

The gunship directed Capt. Lemon to strike the truck. In preparation for the airstrike, the gunship dropped a red flare to identify the target. The pilot briefed Gunfighter 14 to make either a north to south or south to north attack run on the truck. Capt. Lemon said he could not see the flare from the south and would proceed to the north. His Gunfighter 16 was orbiting the area at an altitude of 2,500 feet and his wingman noted he had difficulty in picking up the flare from any direction as he circled the area. The truck was traveling south through the heavily forested jungle with nearby hills reaching approximately 2,500 feet above the jungle canopy.

Gunfighter 14 contacted the gunship when it was north of the target stating that he and 1st Lt. Sigafoos had both the flare and the gunship in sight. Jeff Lemon initiated his first pass on the truck expending his MK-82 bombs. He also informed the other aircraft assigned to this mission that he intended to make another pass. On their second pass, the aircraft was seen by the gunship crew and their wingman to impact the ground and burn in the target area.

The location of loss was approximately 1½ miles north of Highway 165, 21 miles northeast of the city of Ban Phon, the same distance southwest of the Lao/South Vietnamese border and 54 miles north-northeast of Attopeu, Saravane Province, Laos. It was also roughly 57 miles west-northwest of Kham Duc, South Vietnam.

Upon seeing the fireball, Gunfighter 16 attempted to make radio contact with either Jeff Lemon or Walter Sigafoos on the assigned radio frequency as well as on guard channel with no response. Gunfighter 16 then notified King, the airborne search and rescue (SAR) aircraft, giving him the information that he believed his Lead aircraft to be down. SAR procedures were initiated immediately and all aircraft assigned to King flight arrive in the loss area shortly thereafter. Gunfighter 16 continued to orbit the crash site searching for any sign from the downed aircrew until he reached bingo fuel, the point at which he needed to depart the area in order to have enough fuel to safely return to base. During this time Gunfighter 16 was never able to make radio contact with Capt. Lemon or 1st Lt. Sigafoos before departing the area.

SAR efforts continued on 25 and 26 April, but were hampered by thunderstorms. Search operations were terminated on 27 April, and at that time both Jeff Lemon and Walter Sigafoos were listed Missing in Action.

In 1992, a National Security Agency (NSA) correlation study of all communist radio intercepts pertaining to missing Americans, which was presented to the Senate Select Committee on POW/MIA Affairs in a classified format, was finally declassified and made public. According to this document, 3 North Vietnamese radio messages were intercepted and correlated to this incident, 1 in April and 2 in May 1971. The NSA synopsis states: "(The) 16th AAA (anti-aircraft artillery) Battalion; (deleted word) at 1600G, two 37mm guns of Company 3 at the KM-72, struck an F4 flying, expending 10 rounds. Results: the F4 was hit and burst into flames. The (deleted word) pilot was killed, the pilot that parachuted was captured. (The) 16th AAA Battalion; (deleted word) the company shot the pilot while he was parachuting. The pilot is dead."

References:
http://www.virtualwall.org/ds/SigafoosWH01a.htm
http://www.thewall-usa.com/info.asp?recid=47427
http://www.vvmf.org/thewall/Wall_Id_No=47425
http://www.usafa68.org/memorium/im12.htm
http://airforce.togetherweserved.com/usaf/servlet/tws.webapp.
WebApp?cmd=ShadowBoxProfile&type=Person&ID=81509

253

Frank Claveloux Parker III

(Quakertown)

United States Air Force
Detachment 1 (Nha Trang), 15th Special Operations Squadron,
314th Tactical Airlift Wing, 13th Air Force

Rank: Major (O-4) promoted while in MIA status
Length of Service:
MOS: 1575A, Electronic Warfare Officer
Born: March 2, 1940
Died: December 29, 1967 (incident date); declared dead April 27, 1978
Remains repatriated: December 13, 1993
Identified: September 7, 2000
Age: 27
Circumstances: hostile; air loss or crash over land
Location: North Vietnam
Parents: Frank Parker Jr. & Anne (Cooper)
Siblings: 2 brothers (Richard and Michael); 2 sisters (Maryanne and Katherine)
Marital Status: married to Suzanne (Miller); 1 daughter (Deborah), 1 son (Frank IV)

Religion: Presbyterian
College: Lehigh University
Final resting place: Arlington National Cemetery
Location on The Wall: panel 32E, row 96

Synopsis:

Eleven U.S. Air Force servicemen missing in action from the Vietnam War have been identified and are being returned to their families for burial. They are identified as Colonel Charles P. Claxton, Chicago, Illinois; Colonel Donald E. Fisher, Halfway, Oregon.; Lieutenant Colonel Edwin N. Osborne, Jr., Raiford, Florida; Lieutenant Colonel Gerald G. Van Buren, Toledo, Ohio; Lieutenant Colonel Gordon J. Wenaas, Mayville, North Dakota; Major Frank C. Parker III, Bridgeport, Pennsylvania; Chief Master Sergeant Jack McCrary, Madison, Tennessee; Chief Master Sergeant Wayne A. Eckley, Enterprise, Oregon; Chief Master Sergeant Gean P. Clapper, Altoona, Pennsylvania; and Chief Master Sergeant James R. Williams, Charlotte, North Carolina. The name of the eleventh crewmember is not being released at the request of his family. NOTE: Reported to be Chief Master Sergeant Edward Joseph Darcy. On December 29, 1967, their Air Force C-130E Hercules took off from Nha Trang, Republic of Vietnam, on a special mission over North Vietnam. Approximately four hours into their mission, the crew made a radio report from an area near Lai Chau Province, North Vietnam. When they failed to return to base, a visual and electronic search was initiated. About a month later, the search was ended when the aircraft could not be located. In October and November 1992, a joint U.S./Socialist Republic of Vietnam team interviewed five witnesses who had knowledge of the crash site. Two of the witnesses had visited the area of the crash in 1967 or 1968 and provided information about the site. Some of the witnesses turned over identification cards or tags that contained the names of some of the crew members. The team visited the site and recovered some human remains. In February 1993, the government of Vietnam turned over additional remains and a photocopy of more identification media. In October and November a joint team led by Joint Task Force-Full Accounting excavated the suspected crash site where they recovered aircraft wreckage, personal effects and human remains. In 1994 and 1995, Vietnamese citizens and government officials turned over additional remains. Department of Defense analysts concluded from the distribution of the aircraft wreckage that the C-130 hit a mountainside and that the crew was unaware of the impending crash. Nine parachutes were accounted for among the artifacts recovered, and there are no unresolved live sighting reports associated with this incident. Analysis of the remains and other evidence by the U.S. Army Central Identification Laboratory Hawaii established the identification of the eleven servicemen.

All were buried together in Arlington National Cemetery on 15 November 2000.

References:
http://www.virtualwall.org/dp/ParkerFC01a.htm
http://www.thewall-usa.com/info.asp?recid=39433
http://www.vvmf.org/thewall/Wall_Id_No=39460
http://www.arlingtoncemetery.net/oct262000.htm
http://taskforceomegainc.org/P010.html

Epilogue

Rest in peace brave men,
you are not forgotten.

December 2009

Made in the USA
Middletown, DE
10 June 2017